Footprint

# Belfast

Seán Sheehan & Pat Levy

& the north of Ireland

# Contents

# About the authors

Seán Sheehan was brought up in London but spent every summer holiday in Ireland. After adult years of travelling and living in southeast Asia, Seán now has his home in the west of Ireland.

Pat Levy visited Ireland one Easter when she was 19 and the memory of the spring flowers and heather on the hills has continued to draw her back like a narcotic. Author of *Culture Shock! Ireland* and co-author of a walking guide to the island, Pat is now hooked for life and she looks forward to the time when she can tend to her garden in the west of Ireland full time.

## Acknowledgements

Seán Sheehan and Pat Levy would like to thank Fiona Ure and the many patient people at the Belfast Visitor and Convention Bureau for their assistance. Special thanks to Alan Murphy, Sarah Thorowgood and everyone at Footprint who have worked so hard to get this guide out on time. Many other people have helped in our research and our apologies to those whose names we have forgotten to add here: Ruarí Ó'Heára in Derry, Roy Bolton in Bushmills, Eileen in Ballycastle, Maureen in Derry, Michelle McCauley in Bundoran and Ken McElroy in Belfast.

Belfast burgeons in a way that would have been the stuff of science fiction in the not-very-distant past. From a place of deserted, burnt-out and frightening streets to a busy metropolis and hub of culture and hedonism, the city has undergone a transformation in the last decade that beggars belief. The dour Victorian edifices which once loomed over the city, forbidding fun and demanding the Protestant work ethic of all who dwelt therein, are now chic, post modern hotels, trendy bars and temples to the religion of consumerism. The wall murals, which once screamed out the pain and sectarianism of the city's underclass, are now beautifully-maintained works of aesthetic/political significance that feature as stops on visitors' itineraries. No one is more surprised at this turnaround than the people of Belfast themselves. They stand back and wonder as the budget airlines make their city a scheduled destination, as American tour groups make Belfast a stopover, and curious European travellers stand and gaze up at statues of haughty Victorians, gazing back down at them in a mixture of disapproval and avaricious chagrin.

## Dark days

For those of us old enough to remember the dark years of the Troubles in Northern Ireland the prospect of taking a holiday here seems almost ludicrous. Fifteen years ago this city was a ruin: every time a new building went up, someone took offence and blew it away again; at night the gloomy streets were empty apart from the post-apocalyptic armoured cars; and the entire city shut down for two weeks in July when the marching season got underway.

## Titanic hall of fame

But besides recipes for bombs and ranting sectarians, Belfast has also provided the world with artists, scientists, engineers, great industrialists and public benefactors. This is the city that built the Titanic, that created the De Lorean car, that helped discover DNA, gave us C S Lewis, George Best, Van Morrison, Louis McNeice – and James Galway. Seamus Heaney taught here and the surrounding hills inspired Jonathon Swift to write *Gulliver's Travels*. The grand Protestant frock coated men whose statues litter the streets, built schools and churches for the Catholic poor; the revolutionary party of the late 18th century, the United Irishmen, were largely Protestant; and during the firebomb attacks of the Second World War churches opened their doors to the needy regardless of sect.

## Troubles free treasure

If there is a downside to the new and improved Belfast it hasn't yet made itself apparent. Belfast's young and restless earn as much as their mainland or Dublin peers, yet they pay less for accommodation and transport, they breathe cleaner air, they have a spiralling number of cool bars to hang out in and some beautiful countryside at their fingertips when they want to get away from it all. The lively Cathedral Quarter of the city doesn't suffer from hordes of hen and stag parties, the summer is a time for festivals rather than marches and Belfast's citizens reap all the benefits of living in a metropolitan centre without the gridlock and grime of other capital cities.

# At a glance

## The city centre

Dominated by the baroque eccentricities of the City Hall, the city centre is filled still with the grand edifices of the Victorians with their clumsy, didactic, allegorical decorations and pompous red bricks. It is a place for serious shoppers, where all the quarrels of the Belfast suburbs get left behind. It is also rapidly becoming the place to come for very classy restaurants, designer hotels and seriously cool bars. In Great Victoria Street, the very heart of the city, the wonderful Crown Liquor Saloon, the Grand Opera House and the Europa Hotel face each other across the traffic. These three buildings have shared in much of the trouble of the last decades but now all three reap the benefits of the new prosperity.

## Laganside

Next door to the Cathedral Quarter this is where the real success of Belfast's city planners can be seen. All along the river there are bijou new apartment blocks, a long riverside promenade snakes through the city and the two multimillion pound complexes of Laganside Waterfront Hall and the Odyssey Pavilion are making this areas the popular cultural centre of the city.

## The Cathedral Quarter

It has been a long time coming but this derelict area of closed-down warehouses and burnt-out buildings is finally coming into its own. Once upon a time this was the publishing centre of the city as well as an area of linen and whiskey warehouses. In more modern times it has become a centre for off-the-wall artists and community groups. At its centre, St Anne's cathedral dominates the skyline and the new piazzas and urban parks which have replaced the narrow streets and high-terraced buildings which once surrounded it provide it with the context that it deserves. The

## ★ Ten of the best

1 **Crown Liquor Saloon** Have a pub lunch and admire the beautiful old fittings, especially the brass match plates, p42.

2 **The Grand Opera House** Watch a musical or take the free Saturday morning tour to admire the lavish decorations, p41.

3 **Lagan Boat Tours** Take a trip along the river to see the huge cranes, Samson and Goliath and the dry dock where the Titanic was built, p26.

4 **The Ulster Museum** Gawp at the giant machines, admire the jewellery, fiddle with the interactive bits and watch some old footage of Belfast's troubled history, p50.

5 **Ulster Folk and Transport Museum** You could spend a day in this fascinating and authentic outdoor museum, p66.

6 **A black taxi tour** Take a trip around the memorials, murals and sights of west Belfast with the kind of background information that only someone who drove a taxi through the worst of the Troubles can give you, p24 and p54.

7 **The Giant's Causeway** Make a day trip out to the Giant's Causeway, an amazing expanse of natural hexagonal rock formations p85.

8 **The Golden Mile** Have a night out in the Golden Mile starting with dinner at Sun Kee restaurant and going on for a pub crawl around the bars, p138 and p161.

9 **Derry City** Make a day of it in Derry, walking the ancient city walls, visiting the excellent museum and enjoying the craic in the bars in the evening, p91.

10 **Cave Hill** Spend a day out here enjoying the views and wandering its many pathways, p63.

The ★ symbol throughout the book is used to indicate these recommended sights.

remaining alleyways of the area are full of excellent bars, galleries and cafés. Admire the statuary of the Northern Whig and Kremlin, eat out at Nick's Warehouse and study the amazing architecture of the former Ulster Bank. Check out the Albert clocktower, with Albert looking poised to jump if the thing leans any further.

## Golden Mile and the University

This area of the city is where most visitors are likely to stay, eat and while away the evening hours. The university area is home to the Botanic Gardens, the Ulster Museum and the Queen's Festival in Autumn. Along Botanic Avenue, University Road and the streets in between, restaurants lie thick on the ground and genial black-clad bouncers make their presence felt outside every other shop doorway, vetting the punters. Along Donegall Pass and Sandy Row, two last vestiges of the old days, the wall murals and tattered red white and blue bunting, make a last cry for attention as the new buildings go up around them and other ethnic groups with no part in the Troubles settle among them.

## West Belfast

The Falls and Shankill Roads are the two areas where the prosperity of the city has had the least effect. There are still high rates of unemployment and strong feelings of varying degrees of distrust towards the new political initiatives but both areas of the city feel less insular than they once did and in both visitors will receive a warm welcome and be treated to conflicting versions of the last few decades. The wall murals, memorial parks, 'peace wall' and graveyards tell their own gripping story and a black taxi tour of the area is a trip not to be missed.

## North of the city

Passing out through the north of the city you pass more beleaguered estates, abandoned Orange Lodges and peace walls, but moving beyond the urban limits lie the pathways of Cave Hill, the lungs of the city where a stiff walk brings you to Napoleon's Nose with its stunning views over the city. In this area also are Belfast Castle and Belfast Zoo, the latter now well worth a visit with its respectable breeding programme and commitment to the welfare of its animals.

## East of the city

To the east are two of the city's biggest attractions, Stormont, the site of Northern Ireland's parliament building and, 7 miles east of the city, the must-see Ulster Folk and Transport Museum.

## Around Belfast

One of the advantages of Belfast is its proximity to the long stretch of coastline which make up the east and northern coast. To the south is the little town of **Downpatrick** with its cathedral and associations with St Patrick himself, while to the north is the **Giant's Causeway** and the exhilarating **North Antrim coastline**. Travelling west from here brings you to the pretty little walled city of **Derry**, another town which has survived the Troubles and come up smiling. Further afield again is the glorious coastline of **Donegal**, virtually untouched by excesses of the tourist industry with its stunning beaches and quiet villages.

# Trip planner

Belfast shares the rest of Ireland's unpredictable climate – you can experience continual rain in July or enjoy brilliant winter sunshine in January – but like the country as a whole the city rarely experiences freezing weather and is in fact slightly warmer and drier than Dublin, so climatewise a trip can be enjoyed at any time of the year. The best time for a trip is during one of the city's excellent festivals – either the Festival at Queen's in the autumn or the arts festival in spring. A year or two ago there would have been a warning at this stage to stay away from the city in the first two weeks of July, not so much because you might encounter danger but because traditionally that was when people took their holidays, the shops and restaurants closed and the big Orange parades took place. The parades still happen but the atmosphere is more subdued now and fewer places close down altogether. The city is a pretty place in spring and summer and tables outside the pavement cafés help engender a continental mood. But Hallowe'en is a good time too, celebrated much more here than in the Republic of Ireland, with carved turnips rather than pumpkins and lots of events to celebrate the holiday. A lot of hotel prices go down at weekends, probably still a reflection of the old times when there was little nightlife to bring in the punters at weekends.

## A day in Belfast

Begin your day, if you dare, with the full-blown Ulster Fry, a once-in-a-lifetime experience (see page 112). Turn out on to the streets, where the city's rush hour lasts about 10 minutes, and stroll into the city centre where you can take one of the free trips around the City Hall and wonder at its pomp and circumstance, or if it is Saturday, consider a tour around the Grand Opera House – it is also free and a fascinating way to spend an hour or so. Before lunch pop over to Laganside and admire the weir and beyond it the huge cranes of the Harland and Woolf shipyards. Check out the leaning Albert Tower and beside it the oldest building in the city – a pub of course – McHughes. For lunch head back to Great Victoria Street and grab one of the cubicles in the Crown Liquor Saloon, but get there early. Here you can ring the bell and have your grand pub lunch brought over to your table just as they did in the old days. For the afternoon, head out to the Botanic Gardens and the Ulster Museum to admire the huge machinery that once operated in the linen mills of west Belfast.

In the evening the traditional activity is to find a good place to eat in the Golden Mile: Cayenne is worth booking in advance for or, for the more budget-conscious, try out the Beat the Clock menu at Benedict's. After that just enjoy the buzzing nightlife as the streets come alive with revellers and there's bound to be some live music somewhere to meet your approval. If you still need to keep going after the pubs close there are clubs to keep you busy until the early hours of the mroning.

## A weekend in Belfast

Start the second day of your trip to Belfast with a black taxi tour of west Belfast where your taxi driver, who may well have been involved in some of the turmoil which took place in this area over the years, will take you around the murals and other sights of the Troubles. Back in the city centre for lunch, try one of the little pubs in the city's many back lanes: White's Tavern or the Morning Star have good lunch menus and a great atmosphere. In the afternoon head out to the Ulster Folk and Transport Museum where there's enough to keep you interested until you are ready for another evening in the city. This time splash out and try James Street South or Michael Deane's. Then it's off to the Cathedral Quarter where the clubs just keep on partying.

## A week in Belfast

With a few more days at your disposal the rest of the tiny province opens up to you. First stop has to be the **Giant's Causeway**, taking in the picturesque route up the **Antrim coast**, and perhaps stopping off for lunch in the lovely old Londonderry Arms in Carnlough. The day trip can easily take in the Bushmills Distillery, with perhaps an overnight stay at the atmospheric Bushmills Inn, and no-one should leave the north Antrim coast without stepping out across the **Carrick-a-rede rope bridge**.

Another essential trip, if you have the time to leave the city for a day or more, is a journey to the walled city of **Derry**, taking in the city walls, the lovely old Anglican cathedral and the city museum. An excellent way to do this trip is to take the train which goes along the coast to the city, with beautiful views and at a slow, unhurried 19th-century pace.

Back in Belfast, try one of the many walking tours, the Belfast Safari tour or, if you feel fit, one of the cycling tours of the city. A fine place for an evening out is along the Lisburn Rd, where Shu or Tatu offer great meals and a fun cocktail-fuelled, post-prandial session. Or move further out of town to the King's Head where there is always some live music and good pub food.

# Contemporary Belfast

Forget the baggage of the past 30 years; Belfast is a city that is going places. The uneasy peace with its ups and downs of the past 10 years or so has finally and decisively paid off. Two very unlikely parties, whose mottoes – 'Ourselves Alone' and 'No Surrender' – have echoed down the years are helping to plan the regeneration of the city that between them they helped keep stagnant for decades. In many ways the colossal urban decay is an advantage to the newly awakened city. Bomb and fire damage and the abandonment of most of the city's industries has cleared vast swathes of land ready for urban redevelopment. The development of the Laganside area, now well established, followed by the Odyssey complex and the gasworks development have brought new life and much needed jobs to the city.

In some respects, Belfast is a British city rather than an Irish one: familiar British chain stores, the currency, the looming Victorian buildings, the defunct industrial areas waiting for new high-tech businesses to replace the enormous machinery of a former era. Belfast does not have that garrulous nosiness of Dublin or Limerick and it's people are city dwellers in the way that Dubliners never will be. In Dublin people still thank the bus driver as they get off the bus, complete strangers will chatter away, and find they have friends in common, your taxi driver will take it upon himself to explain Irish politics to you, and whole streetloads of pubs will unite in their whooping pleasure while watching the latest defeat of the English soccer team by some third-rate no-hopers. In Belfast, urban survival operates just as it does in any contemporary major city. People don't make eye contact, they choose which pub to watch matches in very carefully, especially Celtic and Rangers games, and outside of their own small areas no-one will stop to gossip to another person. Belfast people seem at first contact abrupt, dour, suspicious even, and given their history why wouldn't they?

Unless, that is, you are carrying a map or guide book, wearing strange-looking European rain gear, looking a little lost. Then you are likely experience another more friendly aspect to these people. Tourism is Belfast's very new industry and city folk are still a little overcome that anyone should want to stand in the Falls Road or the Shankill Road looking at murals. Get past the immediate suspicion and Belfast people, like the citizens of many a big and apparently heartless city, will go out of their way to help, explain and entertain.

Belfast is a city where people are anxious to explain their past to you. It is also a city that is rediscovering that its history isn't just about the Troubles, that it was once a major player in the world, turning out great cruise and warships, and with a huge linen, rope and shipping industry. It seems surprising, given the publicity and attention devoted to the Titanic since the making of the eponymous film, that the actual dry dock where the ship was built has stood derelict, unattended and unexploited. But not for much longer. The Titanic Quarter is just one aspect of the new developments in the city. The Odyssey Complex and the Waterfront Hall have opened up new venues for big names to appear in. And the big names are lining up, all ready to say what a safe, friendly and hip city Belfast is.

And the restaurants! Where once a poor travel writer struggled to fill the pages set aside for restaurants, now the places are legion and the cash just pours in. Belfast's upwardly mobile have joined the cash-rich/time-poor community and at weekends every restaurant worth eating in, and some that aren't, are fully booked for weeks in advance.

If the city centre and the Golden Mile and new development areas are taking off, there are still parts of the city where the wealth hasn't yet trickled down. About 100,000 people live in Catholic west Belfast and 40% of those aged 16 and over are registered unemployed. Equally high numbers of unemployed people live in the working class Protestant estates. There is still trouble at the so-called 'interface areas' where the two divided communities come into contact with one another. The bulk of the

**Hands Across the Divide**
*Noble sentiments in a brave city. Derry has led the way in cross cultural understanding as this statue proudly proclaims.*

new jobs that the tourist industry brings with it are low paid, short-term and subject to seasonal fluctuations. Finally, and ironically, it seems that these two communities, divided by sect, political affiliation and history, may be beginning to sense that they have more in common with one another than they do with the chattering classes who fill the restaurants and never go west.

The two parties, republican Sinn Féin and loyalist DUP (Democratic Unionist Party), which will run the province for the foreseeable future, just as they have been running the city council together for the past few years, will do so even though their declared ultimate goals are irrevocably opposed. The DUP is committed to remaining a part of the UK while Sinn Féin's ultimate goal remains a united Ireland. The population of the province is currently divided between the Catholic population (47.2%) who are largely nationalist and the Protestant population (48.6%) who are largely unionist. Each year the Catholic population increases and will eventually outrun and outvote the Protestant community and everyone is aware of that fact.

Belfast is a part of Europe now and, just like London and Dublin, is dealing with asylum seekers and economic migrants that have taken advantage of the peace to try to make new lives for themselves in the city. Where once Belfast was made up of two cultural groups, both white and Christian, it now has many more, and there are new tensions in the city as people used to old prejudices are learning to deal with new ones.

You are lucky to be visiting Belfast right now. The cities of old Europe – Dublin, London, Paris and their ilk – have had tourists wandering about in them for ever. Here you are special and for a few more years at least will be able to experience a place which has been through the wringer and come out the other side. Its growing young population is no longer moulded by the old divisions, though they are not unaware of what has been dearly fought for, and a population that is politically well educated and socially aware is ready to move on into a more enlightened and equable society.

Belfast's two airports are easily and cheaply accessible from several British cities as well as from New York and a growing number of European cities. Flight connections with London's Heathrow link the city with most other destinations. It is also serviced by several high-speed car ferries from Liverpool and Scotland and by excellent road and rail links with Dublin. Aer Arann connects the City Airport with Cork and the southwest of Ireland. Public transport within the city is reliable and inexpensive and there are excellent bus and train links with the rest of the province and with the Republic. Belfast's rush hour is negligible and parking is still unproblematic, although the city's citizens complain bitterly that all the new building work is taking away the car parks. But Belfast is so small and so uncongested that exploring its side streets and alleyways is most pleasurably done on foot.

# Getting there

## Air

**Flights from Great Britain and Europe** **Easyjet**, T 0870-6000 0000, www.easyjet.com, offers budget flights to Belfast from **Alicante**, **Amsterdam**, **Barcelona**, **Bristol**, **Edinburgh**, **Gatwick**, **Glasgow**, **Liverpool**, **London Stansted**, **Luton**, **Malaga**, **Newcastle**, **Nice** and **Paris**. Fights cost anything from around £30 return up to £100. There are also a smaller number of flights, largely from regional airports in Britain, with **Flybe British European**, T 0875-676676, www.flybe.com, offering budget flights from **Aberdeen**, **Birmingham**, **Blackpool**, **Bristol**, **Edinburgh**, **Exeter**, **Glasgow**, **Isle of Man**, **Jersey**, **Leeds**, **London City**, **London Gatwick**, **Newcastle**, **Southampton**, **Aer Arann**, T 0800-5872324, www.aerarann.com, serving **Cork**, and **bmi**, T 028-9024 1188, www.flybmi.com, serving **London Heathrow**, **Cardiff**, **East Midlands**, **Manchester** and **Teeside**. **Flykeen**, www.flykeen.com, has flights to **Blackpool** and the Isle of Man. **Jet2.com**, T 0870 7378282, offers a daily flight to **Barcelona**, and flights to **Prague** and **Leeds**. Other budget airlines are promising to add Belfast to their schedules in the near future.

**Flights from North America** **Continental Airlines**, T 1-800-2310856, www.continental.com, offers a direct service to Belfast from **New York (Newark)** for about US$500.

**Airport information** **Belfast International Airport**, at Aldergrove, T 9448 4848, www.belfastairport.com, is 19 miles (30 km) west of the city. From outside the airport, Airbus number 300, T 9033 3000, www.translink.co.uk, runs to the Europa and Laganside bus stations every 30 minutes, hourly on Sunday. (You can pick up the bus back to the airport at either stop.) Cost is around £6 for a single, £9 return. Taxis go from beside the bus stop and cost around £24. Some private minicabs are not metered, so you should agree a price before setting off.

**Belfast City Airport**, T 9093 9093, www.belfastcityairport.com, is 3 miles (5 km) northeast of the city. A direct bus service travels from the airport to the Europa Bus Centre every 40 minutes between 0600 and 2150 Monday-Saturday, hourly on Sundays. **Citybus** 21 runs from Sydenham, near the airport, to City Hall. Sydenham Halt rail station is nearby and will connect with Central Station. Taxis from City airport cost around £7.

## Boat

Ferries from the mainland arrive at several locations along the river costing around £150-200 return for 2 passengers with car. Ferries from **Troon** in Scotland (2 hours 30 minutes) and the **Isle of Man** (2 hours 45 mins) both run from April to September only and arrive at Donegall Quay, from where it is a 5-minute walk to Laganside bus terminal, or a 15-minute walk to the city centre. From Ballast Quay, where the ferry from **Stranraer** docks (105 minutes on the Stena HSS and 3 hours 15 minutes on the Superferry), the best option is to take a taxi, while **Ulsterbus** number 256 connects Belfast's Laganside bus station with Larne, 20 miles (30 km) to the north, and where the **P&O** ferries from **Cairnryan**, **Troon** and **Fleetwood** dock. It is also possible to get to Belfast's Victoria terminal, West Bank Road, from **Birkenhead** (8-9 hours). For information on all crossings contact **Direct Ferries**, T 0870-458 5120, www.directferries.co.uk.

## Bus

**Eurolines**, www.eurolines.com, which has a booking office in the Europa Bus Centre, T 9033 7002, operates a service to **Dumfries**, **Carlisle**, **Preston**, **Manchester**, **Birmingham** and **London** via Stranraer.

# Getting around

## Bus

A series of buses radiates out from the city centre in Donegall Square, Upper Queen Street, Wellington Place and Castle Street. **Europa Bus Centre**, T 9033 3000, in Glengall St, has services to **Enniskillen**, **Tyrone**, **Derry**, **Armagh**, **Downpatrick**, **Kilkeel**, **Newcastle**, **Newry**, **Limavady**, **Portadown** via **Lurgan**, **Dungannon**, **Bundoran**, **Ballycastle**, the ferry terminals, and destinations in the Republic, including **Achill**, **Sligo**, **Ballina**, **Westport**, **Galway**, **Athlone**, **Cork**, **Dublin**. The **Laganside bus station** has services to **Cookstown**, **Portrush**, **Ballymena**, **Antrim**, **Larne**, **Coleraine**, **Portstewart**, **Ballycastle** and **Carrickfergus**. There are no left-luggage facilities at either bus station. A private company, **Patrick Gallagher**, T00353-74-9531107, operates a daily service between **Donegal**, **Letterkenny**, **Derry** and Belfast, leaving from Jury's Hotel at 1730 Monday-Saturday, 2115 Sunday, price £10. An express bus service also operates between **Derry** and **Donegal** and Belfast International Airport daily in July and August, Monday, Wednesday, Friday, Sunday September-June, T 00353-74 9548114, www.fedaodonnel.com.

## Car

Car owners should note that while the severe parking restrictions of yore are more relaxed, there are still no parking areas around sensitive buildings such as RUC posts and the courthouse. There is no shortage of secure car parks and most streets have pay and display systems.

Car hire  There are Budget, Europcar Rental, Hertz and McCausland desks in the arrivals hall at Belfast International Airport and Budget and Avis desks at the City Airport. Desks are manned as incoming flights arrive. Rental is per day or per week. See also page 218.

## Taxi

There are taxi stands outside the Europa bus station, and in Donegall Square, Smithfield market and North Street. See also tours below for information on taxi tours of west Belfast. The Smithfield market taxis travel into Catholic west Belfast, taking several passengers at a time for about £1 per passenger, while the North Street taxis travel to Protestant west Belfast. The Donegall Square and Europa bus station taxis have a starting price of £1.50 and do not wait to load up with passengers first.

## Train

Except for the excellent Belfast to Dublin route, trains are an expensive option. There are three train routes out of Belfast: one travels north and then west along the lovely coastline scenery to Derry, another west and then south through Portadown towards Dublin, and a third, smaller line travels east to Bangor. Trains leave from two stations, Great Victoria Street, **T** 9023 0671, and Belfast Central, **T** 9089 9411. From **Belfast Central** trains go to **Larne**, **Derry**, **Bangor**, **Portadown**, **Newry** and **Dublin**, while **Great Victoria Street** serves **Portadown**, **Lisburn**, **Bangor**, **Larne Harbour** and **Derry**. A free citylink bus serves Belfast Central from Donegall Square. The Belfast to Dublin route is very fast and comfortable and costs £23 one way, £33 return stopping at Portadown, Newry, Lisburn and Dundalk. There are no left-luggage facilities at the stations.

# Tours

**Bailey's Historical Pub Tour of Ireland**, **T** 9268 3665, www.belfastpubtours.com. May-Sep Thu 1900 and Sat 1600. £6 including a glass of Baileys. Departs from the Crown Dining Room, upstairs in the Crown Liquor Saloon, Gt Victoria St. A 2-hr walk around some of the city's oldest pubs, hidden away in some of the entries and back streets.

**Drink or drive?**

*Whatever your tipple you're bound to find it in one of Belfast's drinking dens – although not all are as classy as the Crown Liquor Saloon.*

**Belfast Castle**, **T** 9077 6925. Free one-hour tour. Advance booking necessary.

**Belfast City Hall** (see page 32) **T** 9027 0456. Free tours of the building.

**Belfast Safaris**, **T** 9022 2925, www.belfastsafaris.com. Just started in 2004, these are walking tours through the suburbs of the city, covering the Cathedral quarter, Clifton House, Clifton Street graveyard, Crumlin Road and on to Belfast Castle. They offer guided tours or self-guided tours. Phone to arrange a tour.

**Citysightseeing Belfast**, departs hourly from Castle Pl (more often in summer), **T** 9062 6888, www.city-sightseeing.com. An open top bus tour of the city that takes in Laganside, the Odyssey Complex, the old dockyards, the Crumlin Road and the Falls and Shankill wall murals. Tickets (£8) can be booked in advance or bought on the bus.

**Historic Belfast Walking Tour**, from Welcome Centre, 47 Donegall Pl, **T** 9023 8437. May-Oct, 1400 Wed, Fri-Sun. Covers the old town; 1½ hrs. £5.

**Irish Political Tours**, 10 Beechmount Av, **T** 9020 0770, www.coiste.ie. The national network for Republican ex-prisoners organizes these tours to suit individual need. Ring in advance to arrange a tour.

★ **Lagan Tours**, **T** 9033 0844, www.laganboatcompany.com. A trip along the river on *The Joyce*, Mon-Thu, 1230, 1400, 1530. £5. The same company does **Titanic Tours**, another boat ride which takes in the docks area and the locations connected with the building of the Titanic. Fri, Sat, Sun 1230, 1400, 1530. Collect a flyer from the Welcome Centre for a £1 reduction.

**Life Cycle Tours**, 36-7 Smithfield Market, **T** 9043 9959, www.lifecycles.co.uk. 3-hour guided cycle tour of the city. Book at least one day in advance. £12 ( includes bike hire).

**Mini Coach**, 22 Donegall Rd, **T** 9031 5333, www.minicoachni.co.uk. Organizes a city tour and a tour to the Giant's Causeway, taking in Bushmills Distillery and the Carrick-a- Rede rope bridge. Giant's Causeway tour departs daily from Belfast International Hostel at 0930, returns approx. 1745. £16, city tour Mon-Fri 1030, 1230, sat Sun 1030, 1400, £8. All tours stop for photo opportunities.

**Taxi tours of west Belfast** Besides taking their regular passengers into the northern and western suburbs, both the Smithfield market black taxis and the Bridge Street taxis do tours of the major sights connected with the Troubles in Belfast. These cost about £10 per hour and offer partisan but authentic versions of Belfast's recent history.

**West Belfast Taxi Tours**, 5-7 Conway St, **T** 9031 5777, www.jadepro.com/wbta. 1-4 people £17 per hr and £12 per hr thereafter. A tour of the Republican sites of west and north Belfast.

**Black Taxi Tours**, **T** 0800-0523914, 9064 2264 or 078-10033831, www.belfasttours.com. You can negotiate the tour you want. Price is by the hour and person.

**The Original Tour**, **T** 0800-0322003, 07800-918468. Slightly cheaper rate than the rest – £8 per hour but minimum charge of £25.

**Free Derry Tours**, **T** 0779 3285 972, www.freederry.net. The most interesting and educational tour, amongst many, of the city of Derry. The cost is £3.50, departing at 1200 and 1400, and the focus is on the political history of the city. **Derry tourist office**, 44 Foyle St, **T** 7126 7284, www.derryvisitor.com, also runs city tours, departing from the tourist office in Derry. Jul-Aug Mon-Fri at 1115 and 1515, and Sep-Jun Mon-Fri at 1430, cost £5. Bus tours also depart from the tourist office for £6.

# Tourist information

### Belfast tourist offices

**Belfast Welcome Centre**, 47 Donegall Pl, **T** 9024 6609, www.gotobelfast.com, has lots of useful, free information, a left luggage office and will book accommodation and travel for you. *Jun-Sep, Mon-Fri 0900-1900, Sat 0900-1715, Sun 1000-1600, Oct-May Mon-Sat 0930-1730*. There are also tourist information kiosks at the City Airport, **T** 9045 7785, *daily 0530-2200*, and at Belfast International Airport, **T** 9442 2888, *24 hours*.
**Failte Ireland**, 53 Castle St, **T** 9032 7888. *Mon-Fri 0900-1700, Sat 0900-1230, Mar to end-Sep only*. Provides information for your onward journey to the Republic.
**Usit Now**, Fountain Centre, College St, **T** 9032 4073. *Mon-Fri 0930-1700, Sat 0930-1230*. A student-orientated travel agent which can offer tourist information.

### Other useful tourist offices around the north of Ireland

**Ballycastle tourist office**, 7 Mary St, **T** 2076 2024. *Mon-Fri, 0930-1700 Sat, 1000-1800 and Sun, 1400-1800*. Hands out the useful Ballycastle Heritage Trail leaflet that covers a variety of places of historical interest around town.

**Banbridge Gateway Tourist Information Centre**, 200 Newry Rd, **T** 4062 3322. *Jul and Aug, Mon-Sat, 0900-1900, Sun, 1400-1800; Sep-Jun, Mon-Sat, 1000-1700; Easter-Oct, Sun, 1400-1800*. The centre sells a useful little collection of eight route

## Some useful websites

**www.discovernorthernireland.com** Officially-recommended B&Bs, hotels, self-catering, restaurants, plus walking, cycling, golf, angling, diving, tours and an up-to-date calendar of events.

**www.gotobelfast.com** The official website of Belfast's tourist office.

**www.linenhall.com** Irish and local studies, literary tours.

**www.culturenorthernireland.org** Listings and articles on the cultural life and heritage of Northern Ireland.

**www.ehsni.gov.uk** Environment and heritage service.

**www.heritagedays.net** European heritage Open Days.

**www.magni.org.uk** National Museums and Gardens of Northern Ireland.

cards with directions and maps for suggested local walks (including a Brontë walk) averaging 5 miles each and using public footpaths.

**Carlingford tourist office**, T 9337033, www.carlingford.ie. *Mon-Sat, 1000-1700.*

**Carndonagh tourist office**, Chapel St, Carndonagh, Inishowen Peninsula, County Donegal T (00353) (0)74-9374933, www.visitinishowen.com. *Mon-Fri 0930-1730.*

**Derry tourist office**, 44 Foyle St, T 7126 7284, www.derryvisitor.com. *Jul-Sep, Mon-Fri, 0900-1900, Sat, 1000-1800, Sun, 1000-1700; Mid-Mar to Jun and Oct Mon-Fri, 0900-1700, Sat, 1000-1700; rest of year Mon-Fri, 0900-1700.*

**Downpatrick tourist office**, 53A Market St, **T** 4461 2233. *Sep-Jul, Mon-Fri, 0900-1700, Sat, 0930-1700; Jul and Aug, Mon-Sat, 0900-1900, Sun, 1400-1800.*

**Dundalk tourist office**, Jocelyn St, **T** 9335484. *May-Sep, Mon-Sat, 0900-1800; Oct-Apr, Mon-Fri, 0930-1300 and 1400-1730.*

**Newcastle tourist office**, Central Promenade on the way out of town on the A2 to Kilkeel, **T** 4372 2222. *Mon-Sat, 1000-1700, Sun, 1400-1800.* An excellent place to collect local walking information.

**Newry tourist office**, Town Hall, **T** 3026 8877. *Apr-Jun, Mon-Fri, 0900-1700, Sat, 1000-1600; Jul-Sep, Mon, 0900-1700, Tue-Fri, 0900-1900, Sat, 1000-1600; Oct-Mar, Mon-Fri, 0900-1700.*

**Portrush tourist office**, Dunluce Centre, Sandhill Rd, **T** 7082 3333. *Apr-mid-Jun, Mon-Fri 0900-1700, Sat and Sun 1200-1700; Mid-Jun-Sep, daily, 0900-1900; Mar and Oct, Sat and Sun, 1200-1700.*

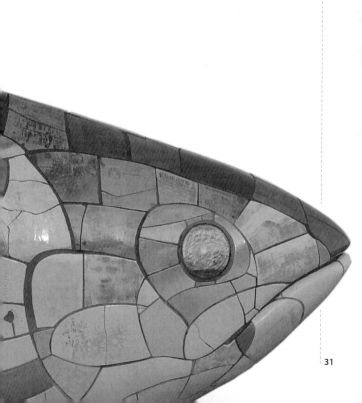

# City centre

*Belfast's central streets are a series of wide boulevards lined with grand Victorian buildings. At the centre of it all is the City Hall, a working administrative building where regular free tours are conducted. Close by are the beautiful Crown Liquor Saloon and opposite it the Grand Opera House, forming an impressive triumvirate with the slightly less beautiful Europa Hotel. Fanning out from the centre are many more imposing old buildings as well as the Linenhall Library. The city centre is also the city's major shopping area and at weekends is filled with families out for the day. At night the streets are quieter but no longer deserted as they once were – designer cafés, bars and classy restaurants now keep visitors here long after the shops have closed.*

▸▸ *See Sleeping p109, Eating p131, Pubs, bars and clubs p157, Arts and entertainment p167, Festivals p175, Shopping p183*

## ◉ Sights

### City Hall

**T** *9027 0456. Tours of City Hall: Jun-Sep, Mon-Fri, 1100, 1400, 1500, Sat 1430; Oct-May, Mon-Fri, 1100, 1430, Sat 1430. Free. Map 2, F/G8, p249*

Dominating the centre of town in Donegall Square is the massive City Hall, a pompous Victorian testament to what money can build. Completed in 1906, the Portland stone edifice, designed by Brumwell Thomas and covering 1½ acres, is topped by a copper dome 173 ft high. You can't wander around inside at will but there

**!** At the time of writing, early 2005, the city council is just about controlled by nationalist groups with the balance of power held by just three people, members of the Alliance party, a cross-cultural group. In May 2005, new elections may change the balance once again.

★ **Victorian architecture**

Best

- **City Hall**, p32
- **Pearl Assurance Building**, p37
- **Robinson and Cleaver Building**, p37
- **Ulster Bank in the High Street**, p39
- **The front of Malmaison Hotel**, pp 40 and 109

are guided tours all year. Inside is an extravaganza of imported marble, stained glass dedicated to various money-men and soldiers, and paintings of various mayors in their regalia. Very few women feature in this place at all, except those who lead the guided tours. The tour takes in the council chamber, the Great Hall, the banqueting hall; and robing rooms.

The council chamber must have seen some amazing scenes over the years of its business dealings. Set out in adversarial style, with a visitors' gallery at one end and tables for the press down the middle. Irish oak panelling lines the room hung about with portraits of people no one recognizes, one of them painted by Sir John Lavery. At the far end are seats once used by the royal family at the grand opening of the first parliament of Northern Ireland which sat here for a while. The scruffy old table at one end hasn't just been left behind by the caterers – it is the actual table which was used by Unionists in 1921 to sign a covenant against Irish Home Rule. You can see a diorama of the actual event in Fernhill House (see p62). Next door are the robing rooms, no longer used since the practice of wearing the ceremonial robes for council meetings was abandoned. The walls of the City Hall are lined with some pretty gruesome-looking past Lord Mayors wearing the great chain of office. Just outside the Robing Room the painting of Sinn

**!** In 1988 an IRA bomb did what German air raids had failed to
**•** do, by destroying the stained-glass windows of the Great Hall.

**City Hall**

*The City Hall, with its gorgeous marble and glittering glass, has dominated the city centre for almost a century.*

Féin's Alex Maskey, the last Lord Mayor, breaks with tradition by showing him in everyday wear and surrounded by images of peace and reconciliation. Most of the rest are dull enough but look for Owen McGuinness, painted by Derek Hill, and Sammy Wilson, looking very laid back and painted by Tom Halifax, the man who painted the Queen (Elizabeth II), wrinkles and all.

The grounds contain more testimony to the doings of men. Statues of Edward Harland, of shipbuilding fame, James Haslett, the Rt Hon Daniel Dixon, Lord Dufferin and RJ McMordie, several of the movers and shakers of the 19th century, all pay court to the quite lissom figure of Queen Victoria, flanked by others who represent the spinning and shipbuilding industries and, perhaps as an afterthought, education. A cenotaph also stands in the grounds, as does a memorial to one of Belfast's biggest mistakes, the *Titanic*, which was built here.

The pediment over the main door depicts Hibernia, Minerva, Mercury, Industry, Labour, Liberty and Industry and some small boys.

For many years the city council was dominated by Unionist politicians who were partly responsible for the failure of the 1985 Anglo-Irish agreement, in large part the same agreement that was made on Good Friday 1998. They refused to take part in council business while the Agreement was in place, effectively making the city unrunnable. A huge banner once hung along the front of the building expressing their opposition to any dealings with the Republic.

## Donegall Square

Linenhall Library, 17 Donegall Sq, **T** 9032 1707, www.linenhall.com. *Mon-Fri, 0930-1730, Sat, 0930-1600. Free. Ring in advance to join tours. Map 4, F/G 2/3, p252*

There are a few other buildings around Donegall Square of some interest. At number 17 is the **Linenhall Library**, which has been a lending library for over 200 years. Although not much to look at

### Organized crime

On Sunday 19 December 2004 at around 2200 three masked men entered a house on the western outskirts of Belfast and took four people hostage. A fifth person, an employee of the Northern Bank in Donegall Square West was taken away. He and his supervisor from Downpatrick, whose family were also being held, were given instructions which led to the biggest bank heist in the history of the UK or Ireland. At 1800 on the following day, one of the men carried £1 million out of the bank in a holdall. No one checked what was in it. Outside he handed the bag to another man. Later that night a white van parked outside the bank and crates of cash were brought out by the men whose families were being held hostage. At 2000 the van made a second collection. More than £26 million left the bank this way, without a single bank robber setting foot inside. Most of the notes were in relatively unusable Ulster Bank stering notes (the bank called in all its notes) but lots of it was in used regular notes. The families were released unharmed.

As with much crime in Belfast, what happened has had huge political repercussions which threaten the peace process. The IRA has been accused of the crime, though at the time of writing no evidence to back this up has been produced. Early in 2005, accusations of Sinn Fein involvement were made by political parties in both the North and the Republic – parties whose objectivity is questionable given that they stand to gain electorally by such accusations. The political fall out continues.

from the outside despite being designed in 1864 by the big guns of Victorian Belfast, Lanyon, Lynn & Lanyon, it has a vast collection of early Irish material and is also used by research students studying the recent history of the Troubles. It is not a public library, although you can wander in and use the reading room and café on the first floor, and browse around the collection of prints that are on sale. The library holds regular exhibitions and talks, and visitors can join one of the many free tours of the building and its collections. The library was established in 1788 and its first librarian, Thomas Russell, was hanged in 1803 after an abortive Republican uprising.

The Square also has some more late Victorian bulwarks of respectability. The 1884-85 **Robinson and Cleaver building** stands out among the solidity: six storeys high with rounded corners rising to ornate turrets, its exterior is highly carved with cherubs, fruit and contemporary figures such as Victoria, Albert and, for some reason, George Washington. At the east side of the square is the **Pearl Assurance building**, built by the same architects as the Robinson and Cleaver building and originally called the Ocean building. It was erected between 1899 and 1902 in a Gothic revival style with oddly-shaped pinnacle towers creating a startling skyline. On the west side of the Square is the **Scottish Provident building** (1897-99) covered in wild carvings of dolphins, sphinxes and lions as well as figures representing Belfast's industry.

## Around the Albert Clocktower
*Map 4, D5, p252*

Northeast of City Hall and close to the river is another cluster of late 19th-century constructions. Now beautifully restored and stabilized, for many years the 1865-9 **Albert Clocktower** leaned a little more with every year that passed and as early as 1879 had to have several bits chopped off that looked as if they might bring the whole thing down. The clocktower had been erected on land that was once part of the River Farsett and over the years its wooden foundations had rotted away until nothing held the thing up but gravity. As the tour guides love to tell you, Prince Albert has

**Albert Clocktower**
*The Albert Clocktower is newly refurbished and, like the city itself, only slightly off kilter.*

**Best**

★ **Picnic spots**

- **Botanic Gardens**, p50
- **Cave Hill**, p63
- The grounds of **Fernhill House**, p62
- **Belfast castle grounds**, p63

**...and  viewpoints**

- **Napoleon's Nose** looking out over the city
  and lough, p11
- The river from the **Lagan Weir**, p44
- The river from **Sonoma** in the Hilton Hotel, p110 and p132
- **Cave Hill** from Victoria St, looking at the profile of the
  sleeping giant, p63.

both the time and the inclination! Beside it the **AIB Bank** was formerly the Northern Bank head office. Built in 1852 by Charles Lanyon in Portland stone and granite, it makes a grandiose statement about the permanence of Protestant values, with giant Doric columns and a great carved frieze above the entrance. In High Street is **St George's Church**, one of the few churches in the city that you can wander into and admire the architecture. Built in 1811 it has a tacked-on portico salvaged from an earlier building, and pre-Raphaelite decorations in the chancel. Along Waring Street, a block to the north of the clocktower, is the now unoccupied **Ulster Bank**, another bygone temple to Mammon and soon to be a boutique hotel. Its architect won the commission

**!** If you stand by the Albert Clocktower and look up at Cave Hill you can quite clearly make out in the outline of the hill the profile of a sleeping giant. It is said that this profile was what gave Jonathon Swift the inspiration to write *Gulliver's Travels*.

Belfast

### ▶ Mary Ann McCracken

Born in 1770, Mary Ann McCracken was the daughter of a Presbyterian cotton merchant, a revolutionary and philanthropist. She attended school, an unusual luxury for a woman at that time, and believed that emancipation should be for all people and not just men. Her brother, Henry Joy McCracken, was one of the leaders of the United Irishmen and led the battle for Antrim town in 1798. The uprising failed and her brother was executed by hanging in the city centre, roughly where the Cornmarket is now. After his death she continued to support the movement for Irish independence and helped Thomas Russell escape to Dublin after the failure of another uprising in 1803. He too was caught, and hanged in Downpatrick. In later life she became secretary of the Ladies' Committee of the Belfast Charitable Society and worked hard to alleviate the conditions of the women and children in the Poor House (now Clifton House). She died in 1866 and is buried in Clifton Street Graveyard as is her brother.

in 1857 in a competition where 67 other architects proposed designs. It is based on St Mark's Library in Venice and has just about every architectural trick known at the time: Doric and Corinthian columns, allegorical sculptures, ornate railings and Victorian lamps.

A little way back down Victoria Street, take time out to admire the façade of the 1866-7 Lytle's and McCausland's, now the **Malmaison Belfast Hotel**, but once two great warehouses whose fronts were preserved with their marble relief figures of the five continents and animals, and arcaded windows.

Back at the clocktower the road sweeps round through some ugly modern road building past McHugh's, the oldest pub in

Belfast, to the **Custom House**, where once the commercial life of the city bustled. Built in 1854-57, it still functions as the city's customs building. Its two fronts, one facing the river and the other the city, are highlighted by ornate Corinthian columns, but the river side is the more elaborate, with the traditional riverine heads as the keystones of arches, and figures of angels, Britannia and Roman gods decorating the pediment.

Also on the waterfront, further north, is the **Harbour Commissioner's Office**, its exhibition of maritime history (including the captain's table intended for the *Titanic*) occasionally open to the public. Enquire at the tourist office.

---

### ★ Grand Opera House

Great Victoria St, **T** 9024 0411, 9024 1919 (tickets), www.goh.co.uk. *Free guided tours of the building start from the booking office, 2-4 Great Victoria St on Wed and Sat 1100. Booking not necessary.* Map 4, G1, p252

---

Great Victoria Street is dominated by the Europa hotel, an ugly place that looks like some brutalist piece of architecture from the era of the Iron Curtain and which was targeted by IRA bombs several times during the Troubles. Also in this street are two Belfast institutions. The Grand Opera House was designed by British theatre architect Frank Matcham and opened in 1895 as a popular variety hall. The theatre is mostly restoration work nowadays after two IRA bombs reduced it to rubble in 1991 and 1993. The best way to see it is when it is in operation – and it is in constant use for concerts, operas and plays. Inside is lurid red velvet, elephant head brackets and a fake renaissance painted ceiling, circa 1991.

! In 1899 a visiting American show required that the Opera House be flooded with 50,000 gallons of water. Later, in 1963, it saw the UK debut of Pavarotti who, understudying in Dublin, travelled up to Belfast to replace a sick performer.

### ★ Crown Liquor Saloon
*Map 4, H1, p252*

The other great institution of this street, on the other side of the road from the Grand Opera House, is the *Crown Liquor Saloon*, which looks like an over-the-top 1990s theme pub but is in fact the genuine Victorian article. It was built for Patrick Flanagan, a publican, in 1839 and later encased in the glorious exterior tiles you see today. Inside are carved wooden snugs, each with its own motto and brass match striker, gas lamps, the original carved wooden bar and beautiful lighting through the stained glass windows.

● *If you are in Belfast on one of its somnolent Sundays, go in around lunchtime when it's quite empty; otherwise you'll have to fight your way in.*

**Crown Liquor Saloon**
*A Belfast institution, the Crown Liquor Saloon has been luring in the punters for generations.*

## A foray into north Belfast

A little further along Clifton Street brings you to a desperate-looking area with an old boarded-up Orange Lodge and closed down churches. The roundabout marks an interface area – a place where Belfast's two opposing communities face each other – in this case the Protestant Lower Shankill Road and the Catholic New Lodge Estate. If you follow the road beyond this point it becomes the Crumlin Rd and on the left you will pass the now disused **Crumlin Road Courthouse** where many famous trials connected with the Troubles have taken place. Built in the 1850s to a design by Charles Lanyon, the building has a commanding Corinthian-style portico whose pediment supports the statue of Justice carved by Joseph Kirk. (Notice, as many of the people who stood trial here must have, that the scales are missing from the statue.)

Opposite the courthouse is the earlier **Crumlin Road Jail** also designed by Lanyon and based on Pentonville Prison in London. The jail once held those awaiting trial but is now home to a new minority group – asylum seekers.

Further along the road again, past the **Mater Hospital**, built in 1900 and once sporting a lawn-covered roof with flower beds and gravelled walks, stands the **Holy Cross Church and Monastery**, built in the late 19th century. More famous for all the upheavals over Catholic schoolgirls walking through Protestant streets in 2001, the Romanesque church has twin towers and a carved tympanum over the doors showing the descent from the Cross. The interior is lavish, with its 19th-century frescoes by one of the monks, brother Mark, plus mosaics and lots of tiles.

# Laganside

*Entirely recreated from the derelict ruins of the city's once huge shipbuilding and shipping industries Laganside is a model of urban regeneration. Pretty riverside walks take you along the multimillion pound developments of the area, through well-designed plazas and dynamic street art. Stretched across the river is the weir which holds back the tidal flow of the river making the upstream banks, which once looked over festering mud banks twice a day, a pleasant place to live and work. Part of the weir is the Lagan Lookout, a tiny museum charting the history of the river and the building of the weir. Walking out across the weir to look at the river and the two great cranes Samson and Goliath gives an idea of what this area must once have been. Crowning the new development is the Waterfront Hall and close by is the Odyssey Complex with the interactive W5, lots of restaurants, cinemas and clubs. Now part of most tourist itineraries is the Titanic Quarter, containing the dry docks where the famously disastrous ship was built.*

▸▸ *Eating p131 and Pubs, bars and clubs p157*

 Sights

---

### Lagan Lookout

**1, Donegall Quay, T** 9031 5444. *Apr-Sep, Mon- Fri, 1100-1700, Sat, 1200-1700, Sun, 1400-1700; Oct-Mar, Tue-Fri, 1100-1530, Sat, 1300-1630, Sun, 1400-1630. £1.50. Map 4, C6, p252*

Slightly more hands-on is the modern Lagan Lookout, a little exhibition centre built on the weir. Part of a scheme to renovate the rundown waterfront, the £14 million weir holds back the tidal flow of the river, which in the past made the area very unsavoury as great banks of fetid mud were exposed twice a day. With the water held back, regeneration of the area beyond it was possible and the place now has a state-of-the-art concert hall, bijou

Belfast is really happening at the minute.
I'm looking around and the people
are looking good, the place is looking good.

*Bono*
*June 2002*

**★ Statues**

**Best**

- Lenin outside the Kremlin
- Prince Albert on top of the Albert Memorial
- The working women in front of the Europa bus station
- The Kelvin Monument in the Botanic Gardens

apartments whose prices are rising at a rate of knots and the jewel in the crown that is the Hilton hotel, one of the first companies to venture huge capital in the newly peaceful city.

The Lookout sits right on the weir and has displays of history and audio-visual material and you can watch the water rising and falling over the bollards which prevent the riverbed's exposure at low tide. A walk across the weir reveals Samson and Goliath, the two massive cranes of the shipyards which are reflected in the glass-walled buildings on the other bank. Self-guided walking tours are available from the Lookout price £2.50 with a £10 deposit. The tour covers the artwork dotted around the river, the new Gasworks centre and the Cathedral Quarter.

● *It is possible to take a boat ride upstream and around the old docks area (see Tours p24). Outside, the ceramic Big Fish is the work of Belfast sculptor John Kindness.*

### W5

Odyssey, 2 Queen's Quay, **T** 9046 7700, www.w5online.co.uk. *Daily Mon-Fri, 1000-1800, Sat and Sun 1200-1800. Last admission 1700. £5.50. Map 2, C12, p249*

Part of the squillion-pound Odyssey redevelopment area beside the river, this is a seriously interactive science and engineering centre aimed at families and schools. There's lots to do and build, handles to pull, things to swing on, throw and bash and plenty of puzzles to solve. There are also interactive displays on most of the technology that governs our lives these days – so can be great fun for everyone. The complex includes a food court, cineplex and omniplex cinema and the 10,000 seat sports arena where the Belfast ice hockey team, the Belfast Giants, play.

# The Cathedral Quarter

*Still in development, the Cathedral Quarter is taking on its own distinctive feel. From the old Ulster Bank, soon to be a boutique hotel, at one extremity to St Patrick's Church and Clifton House at the other, the area is attracting good new restaurants, clubs and galleries. The emphasis in this area is on the small business, and the first people who moved into its empty streets took big risks with their venture capital. But their foresight has paid off. At the centre sits the Anglican Cathedral in a modern little park, one of the few churches in the city open to the public daily. To the north Clifton House has more well established gardens as a backdrop. It is now a retirement home but was once the city's poor house.*

▸▸ *Eating p137 and Pubs, bars and clubs p160, Arts and entertainment p167, Festivals p175*

 # Sights

### St Anne's Cathedral
*Map 4, B3, p252*

Commissioned in 1896, following Belfast's elevation to city status, and built in an eclectic style (the design changed several times even while it was being built) the cathedral wasn't completed until 1981. The nave is the work of the original architect, Thomas Drew and features Irish marble floors marking out the path to salvation and ten corbelled pillars bearing carvings of religious figures. In the baptistery, designed by Drew's successor, WH Lynn, the ceiling is covered in a mosaic representing Creation.

**St Anne's Cathedral**
*The ceiling of the baptistery of St Anne's contains 150,000 pieces of glass and tells the story of the Creation.*

The exterior of the cathedral has benefited from slum clearance over the years and where a guide book of the 1950s calls it 'rather cramped', it now sits in a park area with more open spaces around it. On the north side of the building is the newest addition to the building – a huge Celtic cross on the gable of the north transept.

Travelling north along Donegall St brings you to **St Patrick's Church**, its construction funded by local Protestant businessmen and completed in 1877. The interior contains an altarpiece depicting St Patrick painted by Sir John Lavery.

Further north again brings you to **Clifton House** (Carlisle Circus, **T** 9033 4201, www.cliftonbelfast.org.uk) built in 1774 as a poor house on land donated by the fifth earl of Donegal, an absentee landlord and the biggest landowner in Ireland. The building itself was raised by public subscription and functioned for many years as a laundry. It is still in service today as sheltered housing for the elderly. An exhibition of the building's history can be viewed by appointment only.

# Golden Mile and the University

*The traditional centre of tourism in the city, the area around the Queen's University has always been home to the liveliest nightlife thanks to its huge population of students. This is the area where most visitors stay and eat. The roads leading south towards the university are full of good restaurants and Lisburn Road has become another long strand of places which are worth seeking out. The most inexpensive accommodation is here in the red brick Victorian houses which connect University Street and the Lisburn Road. The Ulster Museum offers a thoughtful afternoon and the Botanic Gardens a quiet retreat. The university itself hosts many events and, while it isn't Trinity College, Dublin, offers an hour's stroll around the grounds.*

▸▸ *See Sleeping p111, Eating p138, and Pubs, bars and clubs p161, Arts and entertainment p167, Festivals p175.*

## ⊙ Sights

### ★ Ulster Museum and the Botanic Gardens

*Museum: Mon-Fri, 1000-1700, Sat 1300-1700, Sun, 1400-1700. Free. Exhibitions change regularly. Botanic Gardens: Apr-Sep, Mon-Fri, 1000-1700, Sat, Sun, bank holidays, 1400-1600; Oct-Mar, Mon-Fri, 1000-1600, closed 1300-1400. Free. Buses 69, 70, 71 from Donegall Sq east.  Map 3, E7/8, p251*

This is probably the least stressful place to visit in Belfast. The museum is laid out as a kind of walk around the interesting features of Ulster with some dinosaurs, an art collection and a bit of geology thrown in. The ground floor is occupied by some massive machinery connected with linen production and steam power. The size of it all is admirable – huge boards set apart from the machines give a description of the process of linen manufacture – but it is difficult to connect the two. Heading onwards on this floor, you find a children's dinosaur exhibition. On the second floor are some exhibits on early Ireland, this time much more hands-on, with video clips, reconstructed huts and other bits and pieces. There is an interesting video on the making of flint tools which accompanies the Ballyclare hoard, a collection of used and blank flints that must once have been the stock-in-trade of a Neolithic flint maker. A display of Spanish artefacts, taken from the *Girona*, a sunken Armada vessel excavated near the Giant's Causeway in 1968, gives a nice insight into life on board, and some odds and ends of ancient Egyptian and native American artefacts complete this level. Finally, on this floor, in **The Irish at War**, the museum gets around to confronting the history of the last century in Northern Ireland. Exhibits are a bit limp but perhaps there's no point in stirring up trouble unnecessarily. What is interesting, though, is the vast archive of radio and TV footage which you can access and which gives a stirring picture of what life must have been like in the worst of the Troubles.

**Botanic Gardens**
*The beautiful lines of the 1852 Palm House sit primly surrounded by rows of institutional bedding.*

Level three is taken up with jewellery, glassware and a wildlife exhibition, while the top floor displays some of the museum's collection of art.

The museum is in the grounds of the **Botanic Gardens**, more of a park than a collection of rare plants but the two long herbaceous borders are beautifully kept and there are some lovely mature trees. The highlight of the park, though, lies in the two beautiful glasshouses. The gardens were begun in 1827, during the 19th-century craze for plant hunting. The 14 acres were open to the public for a fee, but those who bought shares in the enterprise were allowed in free. After 1841 the working classes were allowed in free on Saturdays. The gardens never really became self-supporting financially and were eventually sold to the Belfast City Corporation, which made them a public park in 1895.

The best section of the gardens is the reconstruction of a

**Ulster Museum**
*No surrender! Even the dinosaurs have attitude in Belfast.*

**tropical ravine**, begun in 1889 and extended in 1900 and again in 1902 to include the heated pond where you can see giant water lilies growing. It was renovated once more in 1980. Look out for pitcher plants, tree ferns, bananas, cinnamon trees, papyrus at the water's edge and a great mass of water hyacinth, an invasive weed all over the Far East.

The **Palm House**, completed in 1852, is more beautiful but less interesting inside, being filled with the sort of plants that you can buy in department stores. The designer, Lanyon, used the new invention of curved glass to create the central elliptical dome with two wings. The building was renovated in 1975 when whole sections of glazing were replaced and a new heating system installed.

### Friar's Bush graveyard
Stranmillis Rd, **T** 9032 0202.  *Map 3, E7, p251*

Just beside the Botanic gardens and mostly locked up is the Friar's Bush graveyard, the oldest Christian site in the city. It appears on a city map dating back to 1570 and in the 18th century was the city's main Catholic burial ground. Inside are some lovely old tombstones as well as Plaguey Hill, a burial mound dating back to the great cholera epidemic of 1832. The cemetery was closed down in the 1850s when it became completely full and now only a few families still have burial rights there. There are regular tours of the cemetery in summer or you might be able to get the gate opened by contacting the caretakers.

### Queen's University
University Rd, **T** 9033 5252, www.qub.ac.uk/vcentre. *Visitor centre open all year Mon-Fri, 1000-1600, Sat, 1000-1600 (May-Sep only). Free. Tours can be booked in advance or collect the free Walkabout Queen's leaflet from the visitor centre.  Map 3, D7, p251*

Queen's was established in 1845 as one of three Queen's Colleges in Ireland. It became a fully fledged university in 1908. It owns many of the buildings in the streets around the main campus and the student population of the area has always had a big impact on the nightlife of the place, especially in the years before Belfast became safe for tourists. The university's main attraction is the imposing red brick Lanyon main building. All the grand rooms are open to the public and are well worth a wander round after checking out the visitor centre. There's an interesting guided walk available from the visitor centre which gives much insight into the history of the place.

### Aunt Sandra's Candy Factory

60 Castlereagh Rd, **T** 9073 2868, www.irishcandyfactory.com. *Mon-Fri 0930-1630, Sat 0930-1700, closed Sun. Free. Citybus 32. Map 1, F7, p247*

Slightly off the beaten tourist route in Castlereagh Road is this tiny factory making boiled sweets and chocolates. The front of it is a shop in the style of a 1950s sweet shop. You can watch the honeycomb or chocolate being moulded into shapes and then buy some to take home. Definitely a destination for the kiddies.

# West Belfast

*West Belfast was a working-class area which developed around the linen industry – an area where sectarian violence created two entirely separate communities as far back as the late 19th century: the Catholic Falls and the Protestant Shankill. When the Troubles started in 1969, West Belfast, separated from the city centre by the Westlink motorway, became a battleground. The Falls Road, Crumlin Road, Divis Street, the Shankill are names that ring of riot, burning, assassination and mayhem. However, now a nervous peace dominates the small council estates and Victorian terraces of the area. This is the place no visitor should leave the city without visiting. Bus tours and black taxi tours make the visit easy but it is possible to walk the length of the Falls Road and the Shankill Road and visit all the things to see. The Divis Tower, the Peace Wall, the cemeteries, the murals are all a little too raw and painful to be called sights but beside them are the new community centres, cross-cultural projects, places such as Fernhill House, where you can see the history of the Orange order, or the Bog Meadows where a tiny piece of land has become a wildlife preserve.*

#  Sights

## The Falls
*Map 1, G1/F3, p246*

If a stroll along some of the most battle-hardened streets in Belfast to a cemetery where many of the Troubles' victims lie buried is your thing, then walk along the now-quiet suburban streets of the Falls to the **Milltown Cemetery**, where the Republican graves commemorate some of the many lives lost. The walk begins at the Smithfield market, behind the Castlecourt Shopping Centre, where, if you choose, you can negotiate with one of the taxi-drivers for a personal tour of the area (see p24). Alternatively, head westwards along Divis Street towards Divis Tower, the last remaining building of the notorious **Divis Flats**. The roof was occupied for a time by a Republican group, but is now part of an army post, along with the top two storeys (access by helicopter only). As you walk away from the city centre you can see the 'peace line' between the houses on your right, the iron wall built to keep apart the residents of the Falls and Shankill roads. What strikes home as you walk is the small area of the war zone – a few blocks east and west and only one block between the two warring groups. West of Divis Tower is the 'solidarity wall' where murals reflect the Republican sympathy with troubled people around the world. Its most current illustration is a picture of George W Bush

## ▶ The Belfast Blitz

When Germany began bombing British cities in 1940 Belfast was the least defended city in the United Kingdom. The raids began on Easter Tuesday, 1941, when German bombers rained down incendiary bombs and parachute mines, missing the industrial targets and hitting the overcrowded slums of west Belfast, wiping out houses and the families inside them. Fires engulfed the city, the water mains burst in the bomb damage and there was little or nothing to be done as the fires raged and the bombs continued to fall. Fire engines from the south of Ireland were mobilized and as they approached the city they saw flames rising hundreds of feet into the air. The next morning some of the fires were spent and all there was left to do was dig out the bodies and take them to large public buildings prior to burial: 150 in the Falls Rd public baths, 255 in St George's Market. In total, 745 died and 430 were seriously injured. The second raid a month later caused firestorms around the city including the city centre. Clonard Monastery opened its crypt to the families of the area, regardless of faith. Others had already taken refuge in the surrounding hills and so the death toll was low: 191. By the end of May Belfast was deserted as 220,000 people had fled to the countryside to be taken in wherever they could be while Belfast's well-to-do removed themselves to the hotels of Donegal for the duration. Those left in the city, with nowhere to go and no air raid shelters, took to the hills each night, returning in the morning.

sucking oil out of Iraq. The next stop, about 50 metres along on the left, is a little **garden of remembrance** for some of the Republican fighters from the area who died during the Troubles.

Well worth a tiny detour into St Peter's Square is **St Peter's Cathedral**, designed by Jeremiah McAuley, an architect-turned-priest, and built in 1866. A tidy little building, its twin towers were added 20 years after its original construction. Inside, the major attraction is the newly renovated hammerbeam vault, painted with angels over the choir.

● *St Peter's actually only became a cathedral only in 1986 but at one time ministered to a parish of 25,000 people.*

In Conway Street, right off the Falls Road as you head west, is **Conway Mill**, a former flax-spinning mill which now houses lots of local projects, artists' studios and a craft shop which also has displays about the history of the mill and some mementos of the Republican prisoners' time in the H blocks. From the outside, as pigeons fly through the open windows, the place looks like a ruin; but funding is on its way and it should look a lot livelier soon. In Clonard Street, as few streets further west from Conway and again

**Bobby Sands Mural, Falls Road**
*The murals of west Belfast record the Troubles of the past and the aspirations of the future in this beleaguered part of the city.*

## The writing on the wall

Painting murals has a long history in Belfast. The earliest date back to the beginning of the 20th century, before Northern Ireland came into existence, and were all Unionist in nature. The first one in Belfast depicted the victory of Protestantism over Catholicism at the Battle of the Boyne on 12th July 1690 and featured Prince William of Orange, or 'King Billy', on horseback. These early murals were always associated with the celebrations surrounding 12th July and were part of the street decorations, along with bunting, flags, painted kerbstones and the huge parade. Other paintings included celebrations of the victory at the Battle of the Somme, the sinking of the Titanic, Scottish and United Kingdom flags, and the red hand of Ulster. They became

part of a two-week national celebration when factories closed and everyone took their holidays. Painting the murals was a civic duty and a party in itself. The whole street would turn out to watch the artist at work, making new murals or repainting the old ones. Catholics were of course merely spectators in this celebratory, sectarian, triumphalist parade. Catholic culture was private, ignored by the state and allowed no public statements in the form of murals.

Matters changed when the civil rights campaign took hold. The first nationalist public statement came in 1981 during the republican prisoners' hunger strike. For five years the republican prisoners had taken part in a protest demanding political status and their supporters had taken to graffiti in support of them. By the time

right off the Falls Road, is the **Church of the Holy Redeemer**, or **Clonard Monastery**, which has now entered the history books as the place where the initial, very secret, meetings leading to the

the hunger strikers began to die the graffiti had become murals. They depicted the 'H Block' prison, the prisoners, bearded, rake thin and wearing blankets, their coffins, and the tricolour flag of the Republic. The themes began to extend beyond the deaths of the hunger strikers to what had become an armed struggle for a united Ireland. It was in these murals that the images of hooded gunmen first appeared. As Sinn Féin candidates began to stand in local elections the muralists had more incentives for their work and the murals began to reflect various political and social demands of the nationalist minority and, later, the affiliation felt with other national liberation groups around the world.

The Unionist murals have always been permanent displays – some have been repainted every year for decades – but the nationalist ones are more like graffiti – a mural painted one week may be wiped out the next as some new political issue emerges. None of the muralists consider their work to be art and whole communities turn out with their DIY ladders to do the colouring in with paint left over from redecorating the front room.

In contemporary Belfast the murals are still as important as ever but they have changed their nature in many ways. While many of the murals are still romantic idealisations of the past – the Titanic, the Queen Mother, King Billy, the 1916 Uprising in the Republic – they have also begun to make political statements of contemporary and urgent intent, looking to what might come as their leaders negotiate a shared future.

1994 IRA cease-fire took place. The Gothic-style church was built in 1908-11 and is worth a look for its rose window over the entrance, mosaic depictions of the story of the Redemption on the ceiling and floors and multicoloured marble decoration on the walls.

Next stop along the Falls Road on the right is the **headquarters of Sinn Féin**, its walls paying tribute to Bobby Sands, the IRA hunger striker, and three other party workers who were shot down by a deranged, off-duty policeman who then killed himself.

On the left as you continue is **Dunville Park**, given to the people of the Falls Road in 1889 by Robert Dunville, a distiller. Its centrepiece is a huge ceramic fountain built by Doultons in London.

Continuing on along the road on the left you will pass the **Royal Victoria Hospital**, which dealt with many of the victims of the Troubles. Note its railings which are designed to copy the pattern of a DNA molecule, with x's and y's along the top, just for extra emphasis. Beyond the hospital look out for **An Culturlánn**, 216 Falls Rd, **T** 90964188, a cultural centre and **tourist information** point housed in an old Presbyterian church. It has a café and information on local events.

Further west and on the north side of the Falls Road appears the **City Cemetery**, the city's first municipal burial place, laid out 1866-69. It contains many of Belfast's Victorian worthies and huge expensive testimonials to their own greatness. Look for Lord Pirrie, who built the Titanic, WH Lynn the architect who designed his own tomb and Lord Edward Carson, the Unionist leader. The Carson plot includes a beautiful 1905 Art Nouveau memorial. The cemetery also contains burial grounds for Belfast's traveller community and a Jewish section.

Opposite, on the south side of the Falls Road **Milltown cemetery** is a quiet place, watched over by an army post. In 1988 the war invaded the cemetery when a grenade was thrown at mourners at the funeral of Séan Savage, one of the IRA members killed in Gibraltar by the British army. To find the Republican graves, head south to the end of the graves and then turn right along a tarmac path. Bobby Sands is buried here. The cemetery was created in 1869 and its entrance gate is a typical Victorian over-the-top piece of masonry designed by Timothy Hevey, as is the cross just inside the entrance, but most of the headstones in this cemetery are a much more modest set of memorials than those across the road. One large green space marks a mass grave brought about by the flu pandemic of 1918.

Beyond the cemetery the Falls Road continues into **Andersonstown**, another Republican estate where there are more murals. Beyond that is **Twinbrook**, where Bobby Sands lived, and where a gable end has been turned into a permanent memorial.

## Bog Meadows

Ulster Wildlife Trust, 438 Falls Rd, **T** 9031 4772. *Open 24 hours. Free. Map 1, H1/2, p246*

Squashed between the motorway and the Milltown cemetery are the 53 acres of the Ulster Wildlife Trust's Bog Meadows. Filled with footpaths and ponds and areas of scrub, the meadows are a haven in the middle of the city for a disappearing wildlife. Twitchers will love the place and for others it's a relief from the stress of the Falls Road. Guided tours can be arranged.

## Shankill Road

*Buses 39, 73, 63 travel along the Shankill Rd but not as far as Fernhill. Map 1, E2/3, p246*

A walk along the Shankill Road begins further north from the city centre. The murals are more in evidence here and are slightly more threatening: silhouettes of gunmen and slogans such as "We know who you are" adorn the walls. Typical symbols are the red hand of Ulster, maps of the six counties detached from the rest of the island, William of Orange on horseback, flags (usually the Union Jack and St George's Cross but also the Scottish flag and, both disconcerting and revealing, the star of David), and generally lots of red, white and blue posts, kerbstones, fences, and so on. There are three recent pieces of artwork worth mentioning. One is a recent terrible portrait of the Queen Mother commemorating the attachment that the community of the Shankill Road felt towards the old dear. The other two are gable ends that stand out because they are painted quite beautifully in shades of grey. One, at the corner of Shankill Rd and Canmore St, commemorates the many people of the Shankill who have died during the Troubles and the other, again in shades of grey, makes political comments about Gerry Adams as both a politician and military person, IRA fundraising in the USA and instances of alleged activities being continued by the IRA. Both of them are making a political point to visitors and show an awareness of the outside world that was never there in the balaclavas and threats of the older murals. This last mural stands close to the junction of Shankill Road and Agnes Street which also marks the boundary between two rival paramilitary groups. Allegedly, to the north of the line the drug dealing, robbery and extortion was carried out by the Ulster Volunteer Force (UVF) and to the south by the Ulster Freedom Fighters (UFF). In 2003 the in-fighting between these two groups grew so bad that several families had to be assisted to new homes on the British mainland including their leader, Johnny 'Mad Dog' Adair, who found a new life in Bolton.

Trips along the Shankill Road can be arranged with the taxi drivers at North Street. They should ask for about £10 for an hour (see p24). One possibility is to negotiate a trip out to **Fernhill House** (Glencairn Park, open Mon-Sat, 1000-1600, Sun, 1000-1600, £2) a museum that explores the history of the Shankill area. One section of the museum is a collection of Orange memorabilia – flags, lambeg drums, sashes, bowlers and the like but another part of the museum is dedicated to the details of daily life for mill workers in the area, in the cramped conditions of the two-up two-down housing put up for them.

# North of the city

*Standing just about anywhere in the city the northern hills which surround it dominate the skyline. It was to these hills during the Blitz that many of the Belfast's poor fled each night to sit out the air raids and in modern times it is these hills which provide a welcome break from a city which although small can become overpowering. Two good places to visit, especially for those with children are Cave Hill with its many pathways and picnic spots and the Belfast Zoo.*

##  Sights

### ★ Cave Hill and Belfast Castle

Entrances to the country park are Belfast Castle, Belfast Zoo, Upper Cave Rd. Cave Hill Heritage Centre is in Belfast Castle. Belfast Castle, Antrim Rd, **T** 9077 6925. *Open daily, 0900-1800. Free. If the heritage centre is closed, ask for the key at reception. Citybus 45, 46, 47, 48, 49, 50, 51 from Donegall Sq west.  Map 1, A2, p246*

The north of the city is defined by the high backdrop of mountains, which make up the country park of Cave Hill. Bought up by the city at various times from 1911, the park consists of about 750 acres of parkland, escarpments and woodland. It is grand wandering territory, criss-crossed with numerous footpaths, and is dotted with Bronze Age sites, including the caves themselves (which are man-made Iron Age mines). The best walk of all is to the top of the hill from where there are wonderful views of the city and lough, and even beyond them to the Scottish coast.

Set in the grounds of the country park is **Belfast Castle**, a Scottish baronial pile built in 1870 for the Marquis of Donegall. From a distance it looks imposing enough set against the mountains, but close up it is twee, with too many turrets and curlicues, rather like Balmoral. It almost bankrupted the family, who fortunately married well and were able to complete it. It was

### Belfast castle
*From the ramparts, Belfast Castle, on a hillside above the city, presents a stern façade.*

given to the city in 1934 and refurbished in the 1970s at a cost of a couple of million pounds. It is run now as a series of businesses – a classy restaurant, a bistro, shop and pub all done up in Victorian street style – and is available for hire for weddings and other functions. Inside is a small heritage centre with information about Cave Hill.

### Belfast Zoo
*Open Apr-Sep, 1000-1800 daily; Oct-Mar 1000-1530. Summer £6.70, winter £5.70.   Map 6, F7, p254*

The zoo can be a pleasant day out for children of all ages. It is a vibrant place – and so it should be. It has had around £10 million invested in the creation of new enclosures and general renovation, meaning the animals are well kept and there are some unusual creatures. The zoo has a respectable breeding programme with several endangered species producing offspring. Some, such as the golden lion tamarin, are even put into programmes to return them to the wild. Other assorted animals calling this place their home include penguins, tapirs, spectacled bears and various types of monkey.

# East of the city

*Arguably Belfast's star sight is out here in the east of the city. The Ulster Folk and Transport Museum can provide an entire day of fun, especially for those with children. More sombre is Stormont, the building which is looking ever less likely to be the seat of the Northern Ireland Assembly. The building is not yet open to the public but the grounds are. For those with enough time walking is well worth the effort for its views.*

---

*There are 2 routes east out of Belfast: the A20 goes past Stormont to Newtownards while the A2 passes the Ulster Folk and Transport Museum on its way to Bangor. Buses and trains travel to Bangor and there is the 15-mile (24 km) North Down Coastal Path, from Holywood to Groomsport, east of Bangor.*

---

 Sights

### Stormont
*Bus 16 or 17 from Donegall Sq in Belfast.  Map 1, E12, p247*

---

When Stormont was opened in 1932 it was accompanied by a triumphalist Protestant pageant, but when the post-Good Friday Assembly was inaugurated (see p228), the political balance became a wee bit more level. Presumably, a public gallery will open in due course, but the grounds are always open and the shining neo-classical Parliament building stands at the end of a mile-long drive before a statue of Edward Carson (1854-1935). He

**Stormont**
*Home of the Northern Ireland parliament from 1932 until its dissolution in 1972, and for a few brief moments since.*

was a Unionist leader who brought Ulster perilously close to civil war by using the threat of military action to scupper attempts at Irish independence in the years leading up to the establishment of Northern Ireland.

★ **Ulster Folk and Transport Museum**
Cultra, **T** 9042 8428, www.uftm.org.uk. *Jul and Aug, Mon-Sat, 1000-1800, Sun, 1100-1800; Apr-Jun , Mon-Fri, 1000-1700, Sat, 1000-1800, Sun, 1100-1800; Oct-Mar, Mon-Fri, 1000-1600, Sat 100-1700, Sun, 1100-1700. Last admission 1 hr before closing time. £5, combined ticket to Folk Museum and Transport Museum £6.50. Tearoom. Trains and buses to Bangor stop at Cultra, 7 miles (11 km) east of Belfast. Map 6, F7, p254*

## ▶ Stormont

Stormont, the site of the parliament of Northern Ireland, has become shorthand for the parliament itself. It was established as a result of the Government of Ireland Act of 1920 which devolved all domestic government except taxation to the Northern Ireland parliament at Stormont. When the civil rights campaign developed into open conflict with the Unionist-dominated government, and especially after the British army arrived in 1969, there was pressure on the government to cede its control over internal security. The refusal of Unionism to do this led to the dissolution of Stormont in March 1972. It remained in limbo until 29 November, 1999, when the impasse over the implementation of the Good Friday Agreement was overcome and a new power-sharing executive was formed ending direct rule from London (see p228). Since that time the assembly has been suspended on several occasions, each in connection with the decommissioning of arms, but at the time of writing the prospects of any form of power sharing involving the two major parties seems quite remote.

This is justly praised as one of Ireland's best museums. Dozens of buildings have been transplanted here to form a vibrant recreation of life in Ulster around 1900, complete with staff in period costume. Do not forget to pop into the antique corner sweet shop, which actually sells sweets and marbles and yo-yos. Also worthy of particular attention is the beautiful row of thatched houses rebuilt entirely from an Antrim townland, dating back to the 1600s and lived in until the 1950s. Both entertaining and educational, a visit to this outdoor folk park is highly recommended. A bridge leads across the road to the transport museum where the largest locomotive built in Ireland is just one of the myriad forms of transport represented. The Titanic exhibition pulls in the crowds but there is a lot more to see. Miniature train rides, exhibitions on the history of food and farming, as well as displays of lace making, spinning, weaving and blacksmithing.

# County Down

*South of Belfast, County Down is a series of surprises: reminders of sectarianism in towns like Kilkeel one moment, tolerant places like Downpatrick the next and then, in the blink of an eye, shifting shades of green and purple where, in the words of the familiar song, "the Mountains of Mourne sweep down to the sea". Downpatrick comes alive in March when the St Patrick's Day parade and the associated events are a treat. The old city jail is now a well designed heritage centre. Its ancient cathedral is said to be the burial place of St Pat himself and the crazy Railway Museum is good fun. Newcastle is a busy little town, good for a base from which to visit the area and plan walking trips in the country parks and the Mountains of Mourne while Newry and the villages of Rostrevor and Annalong have their own character and history. In this area is the Bronte Homeland Interpretive Centre, marking the place where the sisters' father and brother taught for a time before moving to England.*

▸▸ *See Sleeping p116, Eating p144, Pubs, bars and clubs p163*

---

*Ulsterbus run regular daily services between the Europa Bus Centre in Belfast and Downpatrick.*

---

 Sights

### Downpatrick and around
*Map 6, H8, p255*

This is a thriving, tolerant little town with several cracking sites to visit, and it is well worth an overnight stay to do so. If you can make your visit on St Patrick's Day (17th March), all the better: you will see genuine cross-cultural celebrations.

In the 12th century, Down was the capital of Dál Fiatach; the real trouble started when the Norman John de Courcy turned up here in 1177 from Dublin with 22 horsemen and 300 foot soldiers.

Down's Gaelic ruler, Rory MacDonleavy, was routed and Down became the first Norman foothold in Ulster. By the 13th century it was the second most important Norman settlement in Ulster after Armagh, with defensive walls and a Benedictine monastery.

Downpatrick gaol saw its share of executions during the 1798 rebellion, when the area was second only to Wexford in the strength of the rebels and the ferocity with which they fought. After this the town went into a decline, which in a way is lucky for visitors, who can see the 18th-century structure of the town almost unencumbered by modernity.

A church stood on the site of what is now **Down Cathedral** (The Mall, **T** 4461 4922; *open Mon-Sat, 1000-1700, Sun, 1400-1700; free; choral evensong third Sun of the month at 1530*) long before de Courcy generously gave back a little of what he had taken in the 12th century. The site is associated with Patrick, who built his first church, and is reputed to have died, at Saul, a few miles to the north. Before de Courcy, there was an Augustinian settlement on the hill. Nothing remains of it, or of the building that replaced it, which was destroyed in the 14th century. In 1609, despite the fact that it was a set of ruins, James I made Down a cathedral, and the bishop was enthroned here beneath a gaping roof. Rebuilding got under way in the 18th century. Inside, it's a cosy little place with 18th-century box pews labelled with the names of their owners on little brass plaques. The organ is built on to a pulpitum, which you walk through to enter the church. The two thrones that face each other across the nave are the bishop's throne and the judge's seat, dating back to a time when trials were held in the church. In the graveyard the remains of St Patrick, St Colmcille and St Brigid are said to be buried. The stone that supposedly marks the site was put there in 1900. In the grounds are several other antiquities, which have largely been brought here from other places.

In the town's gaol is the really excellent **Down County Museum** (The Mall, **T** 4461 5218, www.downcountymuseum.com; *open*

Mon-Fri, 1000-1700, Sat-Sun, 1300-1700; free). There are exhibitions on St Patrick, the history of County Down with lots of fascinating material on the 1798 rebellion, a changing series of exhibitions of art and artefacts, and the barely changed prison cells complete with 18th-century graffiti and some unrealistic models. Sensors along the passages set off recorded prison noises, which can be quite startling if you are not expecting them.

The **Saint Patrick Centre** (T 4461 9000, www.saintpatrick centre.com; *Jun-Aug, Mon-Sat, 0930-1800, Sun, 1000-1800; Apr, May and Sep, Mon-Sat, 0930-1730, Sun, 1300-1730; Oct-Mar, Mon-Sat, 1000-1700; £4.75*) is a very interactive kind of place detailing the life of the saint and the early church in Ireland. Aimed more at local children, perhaps, than the tourist market, this is good for a wander round on a rainy day and may genuinely interest those of a historical bent.

If nothing else convinces you that you are not in the Republic of Ireland, the wacky **Downpatrick Railway Museum** will: only the British are this barmy. (Market St, T 4461 5779, www.downpatricksteamrailway.co.uk; *trains run from Jul to mid-Sep, 1400-1700, Sat and Sun, only, and on St Patrick's Day, Easter Sun and Mon, Hallowe'en weekend, and Dec weekends, 1400-1700; workshop and Station House are open Jun-Sep, Mon-Sat, 1100-1400.*) This museum is run entirely by volunteers and is populated by every crumbling railway carriage that farmers could take off their fields and dump here. One of the trains actually works, and you can take a short train ride to **King Magnus Halt** on a restored, but creaky, steam engine whose provenance will be lovingly described by the volunteer guides. You can also visit the worksheds where skeleton carriages are being worked on, the signal box (carried brick by brick from Ballyclare) and the station house itself (actually the old gasworks building, also shifted block by block). The volunteers have great plans for expanding the line and adding more carriages, and their enthusiasm alone is worth the visit.

There are a good few other things to peer at in this city. **St Patick's** Roman Catholic church (*open daily*), is quite an impressive building: much more modern than the cathedral, Gothic-looking, and set on another hill. It was built in the late 19th century and replaces an earlier church of around 1787. Most of what you see, though, is a modern extension added to hold the increasing congregations in this predominantly Catholic town. Stained glass and mosaic panels detail the life of St Patrick.

In Mount Crescent is a pathway leading to the **Mound of Down**, the remains of de Courcy's fortifications. It is a motte and bailey fortification, and said to be the finest example of such in Ulster, probably built around 1200. Within sight of the Mound, and reached from the Belfast road, is **Inch Abbey** (*free; turn left off the Belfast Rd at the Abbey Lodge Hotel*), another de Courcy job. Built around 1180, it was a Cistercian monastery, and is on the site of a much older place, called Inis Cumhscraigh, which dates back to at least 800. In its 12th-century state, this was a church, with a cloister and several community buildings, including a bakehouse, whose oven was found nearby. There are a good few walls remaining, even though the abbey was burned in 1404, and completely suppressed by 1541.

● *If you are feeling a bit under the weather, go to Struel Wells, 1½ miles (2 km) east of Downpatrick on Ardglass Rd: where there are four ancient wells reputed to have healing powers.*

## Saul

At Saul (Sabhal Pádraic), 2 miles (3 km) northeast of town, is the reputed site of Patrick's first church in Ireland which was said to be in a barn given to him by the local lord. An Augustinian monastery was built here some time after 1130, but today the site is occupied by a Church of Ireland building, erected in the 1930s in the style of a medieval church. There are a few ancient relics in the graveyard, including two mortuary houses of unknown date, cross pillars and a medieval gravestone. Inside the church, the font is 13th-century.

## Around the Mourne Mountains
*Map 6, I/J 6/7, p255*

South Down, between Newcastle and Newry, has a schizophrenic quality. On the one hand there are the majestic Mourne Mountains imposing their granite beauty on the surrounding wilderness, while down on the coast there are unimpressive towns like Newcastle and scruffy villages like Kilkeel. Seen in terms of nature and nurture there is no question about who wins out in this part of the world.

### Walks around Newcastle
For short walks, take Bryansford Road out of Newcastle to **Tollymore Forest Park** (**T** 4372 2428, *open daily, 1000-dusk, car £4, pedestrian £2*) covering some 500 acres at the foot of the Mourne Mountains and with four waymarked trails. Once a private estate, the mansion house fell into disrepair after the Second World War and was demolished in the early 1950s. What remains is a stupendous avenue of cedar trees leading up to where the house stood, which forms a magnificent entrance to the park. The most interesting short walk is the **Rivers Trail** that follows the Shimna River through swathes of violets in early summer before crossing by Parnell's Bridge and returning through forest on the other side. A longer 8-mile (13-km) trail heads into the forest and offers excellent views of the countryside and Mourne Mountains.

Further inland, the **Castlewellan Forest Park** (**T** 4377 8664; *open daily 1000-dusk; car £4, pedestrian £2*) is famous for its arboretum that dates back to 1740, but walking is restricted to a 3-mile trail around a lake with sculptures created from local materials. Enjoy tea in the Queen Anne-style courtyard or bring food to eat in the picnic and barbecue areas.

## Walking and cycling in the Mourne Mountains

Newcastle, with its shops and amenities, suggests itself as a quartermastering base for walking in the Mourne Mountains, and the Mourne Heritage Trust, 87 Central Promenade, T4372 4059, has information and literature on suggested walks. The villages of Annalong, Kilkeel, Warrenpoint, and even Newry, are also possible bases for a few days spent walking the Mourne mountains and all have tourist offices where maps and information are readily available.

Newry and Mourne Council dispense free booklets, *Walking in Newry and Mourne* and *Cycling in Newry and Mourne*, that give lots of ideas for trips. They could be used in conjunction with the Ordnance Survey 1:25000 map, *The Mournes*, printed on water resistant paper and showing all the walking tracks. Also worth getting hold of is the Newcastle local bus timetable, useful when planning a walk between Newcastle and either Kilkeel or Annalong and using a bus to return to your accommodation. Experienced walkers will want to climb to Slieve Donard, using Ordnance Survey Map No 29 in the Discovery series, while a gentler introduction is provided by Donard Park to the south of Newcastle. From here the mountain can be climbed, or you can try a shorter walk by just following the path up the slopes for a hour or so.

From Annalong, the inland roads lead up to the Carrick Little car park from where day walks into the mountains or just along the Mourne Wall (see p76) are possible. From this car park it takes under 4 hours to complete a circular walk up Slieve Binnian, starting by following the Mourne Wall, and then returning along the side of the Annalong River. This is a great day out.

## Annalong

Annalong is a small fishing village, 8 miles (12 km) south of Newcastle, and worth considering for an overnight stay. The beach is too shingly to attract hordes of visitors, and near the harbour the 1830 **Annalong Corn Mill** (T 4376 8736; *Apr-Oct, Wed-Mon, 1400-1600. £1.90. Guided tours*) makes for a mildly interesting visit when a flour-making demonstration is taking place. A coastal path can be followed northwards from here for about half an hour.

## The Silent Valley

A huge reservoir supplying Belfast from the valley of the River Kilkeel was completed in 1933 and its story is told in the Information Centre near the car park in the reservoir grounds. The most incredible aspect of the whole project was the building of the **Mourne Wall** around the catchment area – Ireland's Great Wall – up to 8 ft high, 22 miles long and connecting the summits of 15 mountains. Why it was built, apart from being a massive job creation scheme, is not entirely clear, but it took from 1904-1923 to complete. A 3-mile **walk** by the side of the reservoir is well worth it for the fine views. *Easter-Sep, 1000-1830; Oct-Apr, 1000-1600. £3 per car. In May, Jun and Sep at weekends, and daily in Jul and Aug, a bus service operates between the car park and the top of Ben Crom. £2 return. Coffee shop and craft shop.*

## Rostrevor

The village of Rostrevor has more charm than most of the coastal towns in south Down and nearby **Kilbroney Park** has plenty of open space, riverside walks and an energetic path up to the 40-tonne, pink granite, Cloughmore boulder stone from where there are scenic views across to the Republic, as well as tennis courts, picnic areas and a café.

### ▶ Newry Canal

The River Clanrye and the Newry Canal make an unusual sight, running cheek by jowl through the centre of town. Surveying work for it started in 1703, prompted by the notion of transporting newly discovered coal in east Tyrone from Lough Neagh and out to sea through Newry and the Carlingford Lough. The canal's completion in 1741 was a remarkable achievement. It pre-dated the first canals in Lancashire, England, was built without machinery, and remained in operation for almost 200 years.

The whole canal is now under public ownership and you can walk or cycle along the towpath using the brochure map available from the tourist office or maps 20 and 29 in the Ordnance Survey Discovery series.

## Newry

Newry has suffered from a bad press for years and guide books have tended to write the place off; don't believe a word of it. It's not postcard pretty, but it has history and attitude, and in the coming years could see quite a few changes as the importance of the border further diminishes.

Nowadays Newry is at peace, and while there are no special attractions it is a most interesting place to wander around (free town map from the tourist office) because the lack of developments over the last 30 years has helped preserve examples of industrial architecture that will soon no doubt succumb to the bulldozer. It is well worth using the **Newry Heritage Trail**, available from the tourist office, for a self-guided tour. There is also the waymarked **Newry Canal Way**, a 20-mile cycling and walking route connecting Newry with Portadown that follows the towpath of the now non-navigable Newry Canal. A guide to the Way is available from the tourist office.

Right next to the tourist office, where a town map is available, stands the magisterial **town hall**. It dates from 1893, built on a bridge near where the road from Armagh becomes Canal Street and meets Merchants Quay by the side of the canal. Tucked away behind it is a more interesting example of late-Victorian building, a five-storey brick-built structure with three arched doorways built in 1879. An even better example of Victorian industrial architecture can be admired by leaving the town hall and walking away from the town centre and across the junction with Canal Street to **Sand's Mill** in New Street: seven floors of red and yellow bricks, arcaded, and still in use since it first opened to business in 1873.

### The Brontë Homeland

The tourist board has made the best out of the least interesting part of Down by dubbing an area to the south of Banbridge, about half-way between Newry and Belfast, the 'Brontë Homeland', as it was here that Patrick Brontë, father of the famous literary family, lived and worked before moving to Haworth in Yorkshire. If travelling south to Banbridge from Belfast, the Georgian-style town of **Hillsborough** offers a touch of genteel elegance: break here for tea and cakes. Alternatively, push on for Banbridge and head for the tourist information centre (see p28).

The first stop on a Brontë tour should be the **Brontë Homeland Interpretative Centre** (Drumballyroney Church and School House near Rathfriland, 8 miles from Banbridge off the B10, Church Hill Rd, **T** 4063 1152. *Open Mar-Sep, Tue-Fri, 1100-1700; same hours Oct-Feb but closed Mon. £2*). Patrick Brontë and the novelist sisters' brother, Bramwell, taught and preached here. A free leaflet  with a map outlines a tour that takes in four other sites associated with the Brontës' father and provides as good a reason as any for threading one's way through a little-visited part of Down.

# Dundalk and the Cooley Peninsula

*Dundalk in the Republic's County Louth and midway between Belfast and Dublin, is a lively, underestimated town. Once tagged as a border town of ill-repute, it is justifiably fed up with tired clichés from the past and for visitors who appreciate a town unsullied by mass tourism smart Dundalk is a place to see and savour. The Cooley Peninsula is a great place for walks; there's the Táin Way for those who like waymarked routes but also lots of shorter, less well travelled routes. Here too is Carlingford, unspoiled by tourism where you can visit a heritage centre and some medieval remains.*

▸▸ *See Sleeping p119 and Eating p146 and Pubs, bars and clubs p163, Sports p195*

---

*There are direct bus and train services to Dundalk from Belfast. On the Dublin to Belfast rail line there are at least seven trains a day in either direction, and four on Sundays. There are regular bus services hourly or more from Belfast to Dundalk, many of them involving changing buses at Newry. Journey time is between 1 hour 10 minutes and 1 hour 30 minutes.*

---

## ◉ Sights

---

### Dundalk
*Map 6, J5, p255*

---

A short walk around town takes in the most interesting buildings but if you have the time collect the free Heritage Trail map from the tourist office (see p30) and follow the longer self-guided walk it describes.

International direct dialling to the Republic of Ireland: 00353.
Local Dundalk area code: (0)42.

Starting outside the tourist office, the **County Museum** (**T** 042-9327056, *Mon-Sat, 1030-1730, Sun 1400-1800*, €3.80) is next door in a restored 18th-century warehouse and houses two new floors, one devoted to archaeology and early history and the other to Norman and medieval history.

Walk down Jocelyn Street, past the tourist office, to the road junction; don't turn directly right into Chapel Street but head for Crowe St, the right fork along Roden Place, pausing before you do so to admire the art nouveau **Century Bar** on the corner. Built to celebrate the beginning of the 20th century, original features of its design have been retained and are worth appreciating over a morning drink. Crowe Street leads past the Greek-style **Courthouse**, one of the finest examples of a 19th-century courthouse in Ireland, on the corner of Market Square. Doric columns cut from white Portland stone and the granite ashlar blocks of the stern flanking walls of this still functioning courthouse proclaim a Spartan rather than Athenian sense of justice.

Head up Clanbrassil Street from Market Square, passing the superb example of Victorian commercial architecture at No 70, to where **St Nicholas' Church** stands on the right just past Yorke Street. A mishmash of architectural styles, the churchyard has the grave of Agnes Galt, sister of the poet Robert Burns, who lived just outside of town for nearly 20 years. Continue along Yorke Street and turn right into Chapel Street to return to the Century Bar.

## Cooley Peninsula
*Map 6, J6, p255*

Nestled between Dundalk Bay and Carlingford Lough (a true fjord), the Cooley Peninsula and the view across to the Mourne Mountains never looks better than on a soft day when a gentle mist shrouds the land. The area's association with a rich vein of

Irish mythology then seeps through the landscape evoking the tales of Cú Chulainn who, in just one of his adventures, had to cope with the magic of Morrígan in the triple guise of a red-eared heifer, a she-wolf and a black eel. More down to earth in every sense of the word is Carlingford, a village that retains its medieval heritage to a remarkable degree yet risks mutation into an overpriced, Kinsale-like consumer den.

## Walking in the steps of Cú Chulainn

With a copy of Kinsella's translation of *The Táin* and Ordnance Survey sheet 29 in the Discovery Series, a day or even an entire holiday could be spent walking the hills between Carlingford and Omeath. The **Táin Way**, a 25-mile (40-km) waymarked walking route, is one possibility (though restricted to asphalt too much of the time) and the tourist office in Carlingford (see p29) sells *The Táin Way Map Guide* with a 1:50,000 scale map. *Rambles* is a booklet with simple maps that briefly describes nearly a dozen walks that all begin from Carlingford and last from one to six hours. With just the OS map you can devise your own route: start, for example, on the Táin Way, and head off for the **Windy Gap**, *Bernas Bo Ulad* in the saga, and the setting for a much later love tragedy featuring the death of a Spanish woman who was brought here after being deceived into thinking she had a rich land to inhabit.

A **recommended 12-km walk** (OS map essential) is a circular route from Ravensdale up the Black Mountain to Clermont Cairn (1675 ft; 510 m), along the Táin Trail and through Ravensdale Forest to the R174 road. Between May and August a flower guidebook would be useful.

## Medieval Carlingford

What makes Carlingford special is that this medieval town remained largely unchanged throughout the 1960s and 1970s, when the rest of Ireland was reinventing and repackaging itself for Nostalgia Inc. It still has the feel of an unmolested little corner of Ireland and there are marvellous medieval remains: the **Mint** in Tholsel Street, with its machicolated and carved limestone windows, **King John's Castle** by the lough, and the **Tholsel**, a surviving gate. In the **Holy Trinity Heritage Centre** (Churchyard Rd, **T** 042-9373454, *mid-Mar to Sep, daily, 0930-1700*); a mural, video and exhibitions tell the history.

# North Antrim Coast

*The scenic northern coastline of the province is its most tourist orientated area but those who fear the heritage centre/tour bus brigade need not worry. Bushmills Distillery and the Giant's Causeway are busy but still avoid the worst excesses of mass catering. At the Causeway in particular it is easy to get away from the crowds around the visitor centre and explore the strange rock formations. The Carrick-a-rede rope bridge is good if you have nerves of steel and Ballycastle and the busy little seaside town of Portrush each offer their own delights. Rathlin Island, close to Ballycastle provides fresh air, excellent walks and wild birds to spot. The Ulster Way passes through the area for those who enjoy waymarked walks while local tourist offices have details of many shorter, less obvious routes.*

▸▸ *See Sleeping p121, Eating p148, Pubs, bars and clubs p165*

---

***Public transport along the North Antrim coast*** *Between 31 May and 25 Sep the Ulsterbus 252 Antrim Coaster,* **T** *9066 6630, www.translink.co.uk, service runs daily between Belfast and Coleraine, stopping at all the main towns of interest. Buses leave Belfast at 0900 (leaving Coleraine at 0955) and stop at Portrush, Portballintrae, Bushmills, Giant's Causeway, Ballintoy, Ballycastle, Cushendun, Cushendall, Carnlough, Glenarm, Larne, Carrickfergus and Belfast.*

*In July and August there is an open-topped bus, service number 177, the Bushmills Open Topper running 5 times a day between*

*Coleraine and the Causeway, via Portstewart, Portrush, Portballintrae and Bushmills, but flaggable anywhere along its route.*

*The Ulsterbus 152 service runs between Ballycastle and Portrush on the B146, via Carrick-a-rede, Ballintoy and the Giant's Causeway.*

*The Causeway Rambler, service number 402, operates daily, 7 times a day from Bushmills Distillery (1015-1700) and from Carrick-a-rede (1045-1730) between early June and early September, calling at the Giant's Causeway, Dunseverick Castle, White Park Bay, Ballintoy and Carrick-a-rede. An all-day, hop on and hop off ticket costs £3.50.*

#  Sights

## Portrush
Map 6, B4, p254

Portrush, is a busy seaside resort packed with activities for families, and while the downside may be the usual tackiness and the excess of buckets and spades dangling from shop doorways, there are upbeat surprises in store as well, for Portrush is a superb centre for surfing.

**Curran Strand** is the sandy beach, that stretches eastwards for over a mile, past the famous golf course, to the **White Rocks**, perfect for picnics, where erosion has weathered and sculptured arches and caves into weird shapes. Surfing is good here: try the East Strand, which can be reached by car, although the West Strand is just as good.

The **Ulster Way** path, rising up to clifftop level, follows the coast from Portrush to Portstewart. From Portrush Harbour, **boat trips** head out to tour The Skerries, a chain of small islands off the coast. Horse riding is also an option: see p198.

The **Dunluce Centre** and **Waterworld** by the harbour, are two attractions worth taking the kids to, see pages 214 and 215.

## Dunluce Castle

Beside the A2, Portballintrae, **T** 2073 1938. *Open Apr-May and Sep, Mon-Sat, 1000-1800, Sun, 1400-1800; Jun-Aug, Mon-Sat, 1000-1830, Sun, 1200-1600; Oct-Mar, Tue-Sat, 1000-1600, Sun, 1400-1600. £1.50. Visitor Centre, guided tours. Map 6, B4, p254*

The castle at Dunluce, one of the most enjoyable to visit anywhere in Ireland, is not one of those brutal Norman impositions, for there is something whimsical as well as dramatic about its spectacular location on a rock-stack. There's been a fortification of some kind here for perhaps as long as two millennia but the earliest of the castle walls were built in the 14th century for the MacQuillans, Scottish mercenaries originally, and completed later by the MacDonnells. The English under Sir John Perrott, determined to clear the Scots from Antrim, took the castle with artillery in 1584, but the following year Sorley Boy MacDonnell and his men scaled the cliffs on ropes and hung the constable (his Scots mistress is said to have played an invaluable part in this). Perrott was philosophical: "I do not weigh the loss but can hardly endure the discredit". The MacDonnells made a deal and remained the residents and their subsequent repair work lasted 60 years until the kitchen and servants' quarters collapsed into the sea and ruined a perfectly good night's dinner. There is plenty of the castle left standing and a visit is recommended.

## Bushmills Distillery

**T** 2073 1521, www.bushmills.com. *Open Apr-Oct, Mon-Sat 0930-1730, Sun 1200-1730, last tour at 1600; Nov-Mar, Mon-Fri, tours on the hour between 1030 and 1530 (but not 1230). £3.95. Nearest tourist information at the Giant's Causeway, T 2073 1855.*

Bushmills developed with the rise of water-powered industry in the early 17th century – the first hydro-electric tramway in the world came through here on its way from Portrush to the

### Bushmills whiskey distillery
*Visitors come from all over the world to this quiet little town in County Antrim where the famous whiskey is made.*

Causeway – and whiskey was first legitimately distilled here in 1608. A guided tour of The Old Bushmills Distillery covers history and technology and finishes with the customary taster of the famous single malt (triple-distilled) whiskey.

● *Bushmills makes a convenient watering hole for lunch, before or after a visit to the Causeway.*

---

### ★ Giant's Causeway
Giant's Causeway Centre, **T** 2073 1582. *Open Jul-Aug, daily 1000-1900. Shorter hours rest of the year. Audio-visual show £1. Car park £5. Tea-room open mid-Mar to Nov. There is no charge to visit the Giant's Causeway unless arriving by car or wishing to hop in the minibus, £2 return, from the Causeway Centre to the shore. Map 6, A5, p254*

Formed by the cooking and cooling of vast quantities of basalt, the giant crystals of the Giant's Causeway have been attracting countless visitors since they were first 'discovered' by the Victorians. The novelist Walter Scott selected four of the basalt columns to take home with him but changed his mind, the poet Keats set out to walk here from Donaghadee but found it too long a journey, while Thackeray in his 1842 tour was led to exclaim that when God fashioned the world out of chaos "this must have been *the bit over* – a remnant of chaos".

One version has it that the polygonal columns were spewed forth as the result of a cataclysmic convulsion in the crust of oceanic tectonic plates, but the Causeway Centre is not bound by modern dogma and the exhibition allows visitors to choose between this prosaic account and the rather more fanciful story about lusty Finn McCool (Fionn Mac Cumhaill), who wanted a passageway across the water to reach a giantess on the island of Staffa, off the coast of Scotland. (This is backed up by science, for similar rock formations are indeed found there as well.)

Once you leave behind the rather tasteless interpretive centre and actually see the rocks you can understand what has been bringing so many people here over the years. It really does seem as though some bad-tempered giant had set the rocks down here in an ugly fit of pique.

From the Causeway Centre it is a short walk to the shore and Finn's stepping stones, but in summer you will have to dodge minibuses and hordes of visitors. Follow instead the path up behind the Centre and take the **North Antrim Cliff Path**; a few hundred steps bring you down to the shore.

### Walking the Causeway coast

Having ticked off the Giant's Causeway on your 'been there, done that' list, it seems a pity to leave the majestic North Antrim coast too quickly, and luckily the Causeway Coast Way (North Antrim Cliff Path) provides an exhilarating way of extending one's stay. It takes about five hours to walk the 17 km (10 miles) between Portballintrae and Ballintoy, and with the aid of a timetable it should be possible to catch a bus (see p82) back to your vehicle or accommodation. While the path (*Ordnance Survey map 5, Discoverer series*) can be walked in either direction, the best fun can be had if you start from Ballintoy and cross White Park Beach to the little harbour of Portbraddan, where St Gobhan's claims to be the smallest church in Ireland, and on to Dunserverick and up to the clifftop for a spectacular couple of miles to the Giant's Causeway. Walking in Northern Ireland doesn't come much better than this.

**Giant's Causeway**
*Basalt crystals thrown up by shifting tectonic plates or a giant's personal footpath; either way, the Giant's Causeway is a wonder.*

● *The tourist office in Portrush has a leaflet describing a walk following the tracks of the Causeway Tram that ran between Portrush and the Causeway between 1883 and 1949. There is talk of relaying part of the line.*

## Carrick-a-rede

**T** 2073 1582. *Open (weather permitting) mid-Mar to Jun and Sep, daily 1000-1800; Jul-Aug, daily 1000-1900. £2. Centre and tea-room: Jun-Aug and weekends in May, daily 1200-1800. Map 6, B5, p254*

Every year some 100,000 visitors cross the rope bridge at Carrick-a-rede but that may prove scant comfort when you are halfway across and you realize that turning back means going as far as carrying on to the other side. It's only 80 ft (24 m) above the sea, but when the rope bridge starts to sway and your nerves wither, try to remember that you're just on holiday – having fun. The bridge is erected annually by fishermen throwing a string across with a lead weight to access a salmon fishery on the small island. The centre by the car park has information panels on the geology and the quarrying in the 1930s-50s that removed the entirety of Larrybane Head and the remains of a promontory fort.

## Ballycastle
*Map 6, B5, p254*

Ballycastle is a modestly vivacious little place with some history and a character reminiscent of the Republic. There are pubs with traditional music, fair restaurants and an infrastructure that recommends it both as a base for exploring the North Antrim coast and as a place to pause before or after seeing the Glens of Antrim on the east coast. Northern Ireland's only inhabited island (Rathlin Island) lies off the coast, Scotland is a short ferry ride away, and every year three festivals light up the place with song, dance and live music on a stage in the Diamond.

**Carrick-a-rede**
*Carrick-a-rede island is accessible only during the summer via a terrifying 60 ft long rope bridge slung across from the mainland.*

### Walking around Ballycastle
The Ulster Way passes through Ballycastle but the route west of town is not recommended until Ballintoy is reached (see Walking the Causeway coast on p86). While the route east is a tough hike of 20 miles (32 km) to Cushendall, a more manageable trek could end in Cushendun and would take in a glorious clifftop walk around Fair Head and the ascent of Carnanmore (1,243 ft/379 m). You need *Ordnance Survey* maps 5 and 9 in the Discoverer series.

For gentle strolls collect the *Forest Walks* leaflet from the tourist office (see p28) which maps out the circular 2-mile **Glentaisie Trail** and the 3-mile **Glenshank Trail**, both waymarked.

### Cushendall
*Overlooked by the flat topped Lurigethan Hill, Cushendall is a busy little holiday village in the Glens of Antrim*

### Rathlin Island
*Caledonian MacBrayne, **T** 2076 9299, run the M.V. Canna Ferry on its 45-minute journey to Rathlin four times a day between Jun and Sep (1000, 1200, 1630, and 1830, or 1900 on Fri), and twice a day the rest of the year. Day return £8.60, bicycles can be hired for £2 and are best booked ahead in the summer. Map 6, A5/6, p254*

Just 6 miles (9.6 km) from Ballycastle and 14 miles (22.5 km) from the Mull of Kintyre in Scotland, Rathlin has an inverted L-shape, 4 miles by 3 (6.5 by 4.8 km), and is never wider than a mile (1.6 km). Collect a brochure with map from the tourist office in Ballycastle (see p28) and jump on the ferry for a day out in the fresh air.

Famous people come to Rathlin. The Vikings started their tour of Ireland here in 795. Half a century later, Robert the Bruce, in hiding after a whipping by the English at Perth, was inspired by a spider to never give in, and left to fight the English again at Bannockburn.

Sir Francis Drake commanded a ship sent here in 1575 to hunt down the family and friends of Sorley Boy MacDonnell and massacre them. Marconi, or at least his assistant, sent the world's first wireless message here from Ballycastle in 1891, and around a century later the capitalist Richard Branson came down in a balloon near here.

**Walking** and **birdwatching** are the main attractions of a visit, and there is a viewing platform (**T** 2076 3948, *Apr-Aug*) at the West Lighthouse. In late spring and early summer the rocks are crowded with fulmars, guillemots, kittiwakes, Manx shearwaters, razorbills and puffins.

**Diving** trips can be arranged, **fishing** off the rocks is possible and boats can also be hired. Colonies of grey and common seals can be seen at Mill Bay, just south of the harbour and near the hostel and camping ground, and at Rue Point near the South Lighthouse (**T** 2076 3948).

# ★ Derry

*Derry is a lovely, compact, vibrant little city, full of business and bustle, where life has moved on from the Troubles but without turning its back on the suffering and sacrifices endured by its citizens in the past. Highlights of a visit include the intact 17th-century walls and the equally ancient cathedral. The modern Tower Museum is a model of well balanced and fascinating storytelling and the well-run tourist office offers excellent tours of the Bogside which give you an idea of the city's turbulent history, as well as the more traditional tours of the city walls and architecture. Derry's a place you won't want to leave so if you have time plan for at least an overnight stay. There is music in the bars at night, some good restaurants offer exciting food and the number of quality hotels grows every year.*

▸▸ *See Sleeping p124, Eating p150, Pubs bars and clubs p166*

*Derry is a very accessible city. The airport, **T** 7181 0784, www.cityofderryairport.com, is 7 miles (11 km) northeast of the city on the A2, and access to the city is by Ulsterbus service 143 or taxi. Derry's Waterside railway station, **T** 7134 2228, is on the eastern side of the River Foyle , and there is a free bus service to and from the Ulsterbus Depot in Foyle St.*

*Local buses begin their journeys at the Ulsterbus depot: they are indicated by the letter 'D' in front of the service number. Black taxis wait at Foyle St and collect a full load of passengers before setting off. Regular cabs operate around the city; ask the price before you set off, since few have meters.*

##  Sights

The city centre of Derry can easily be experienced in a day's wander around the walls, dropping down into the city to visit the various sights. The sights of Derry, as set out below, take in a clockwise walk of the city walls beginning at Shipquay Gate.

### The city walls
*Map 5, C-F 1-5, p253*

Considering Derry's history, it is amazing the walls are intact: two-storey ramparts of earth and stone a mile long with a wide protected walkway along their top. Starting the walk at Shipquay Gate, one can imagine the 17th-century walled town. The gate had a drawbridge that could be closed against attackers and the river lapped against the walls themselves.

Inside Shipquay Gate there are steps up on to the wall, which you can follow in a clockwise direction. At regular intervals bastions project out beyond the walls; they were used as defensive positions when the city was under attack. Beyond the third gate, **New Gate**, the Church of Ireland cathedral comes into view with its tower projecting above the walls. During the siege of Derry the tower was given wooden platforms for the defenders to use. The walls around the church are built higher than usual, again as a defensive measure during the siege. Beyond the church and outside the walls is the Fountains area, distinguished by its red, white and blue decorations.

Approaching **Bishop's Gate** you can see the one remaining tower of the old Derry jail which has a long list of famous inmates including Wolf Tone, the leader of the United Irishmen, and Eamon de Valera, later president of Ireland. Descending by the Bishop's Gate, notice the carved ornamentation on the gate, which is built like a triumphal arch, rebuilt in 1789 to honour William of Orange. After its construction a united procession of church leaders passed through the gate (in those days William of Orange represented order, not sectarianism). Passing along Bishop's Gate Within you pass the pink, columned **Bishop's Palace** on the left where Cecil Frances Alexander, the wife of a later bishop lived, famous for writing a collection of hymns for children including those old favourites *There is a Green Hill* and *All Things Bright and Beautiful*. On the right is the **courthouse**, which suffered three car bomb attacks and was restored in 1994. Turning right brings you past the Irish Society (The Honourable) houses where the clergy live and into the grounds of the Cathedral.

### St Columb's Cathedral

**T** 7126 7313, www.stcolumbscathedral.org. *£1.50. Open Mar-Oct, Mon-Sat, 0900-1700; Nov-Feb, Mon-Sat, 0900-1300, 1400-1600. Map 5, F3, p253*

The cathedral was built by the Irish Society between 1628 and 1633 and is one of the few churches in Ireland that is in a single style – late Gothic. The spire is the church's third – the first was wooden and was pulled down in preparation for the siege (see p224), the lead being used to make bullets; another spire went up

### ▶ Derry's part in the Troubles

In October 1968 civil rights marchers in Derry including John Hume, Gerry Fitt (both leaders of the moderate SDLP) and three Westminster Labour MPs were trapped by police and bludgeoned till they fled. Fitt was taken to hospital with head injuries. The event was filmed by an Irish film crew and broadcast worldwide – Ulster policemen were seen randomly hitting out at demonstrators and bystanders alike. This event was the trigger that sent Northern Ireland spiralling into the Troubles. Prior to this, the RUC had commanded the respect of the minority communities in Northern Ireland; after this they lost it.

By 1969 the civil rights movement had grown, become largely Catholic and contained Socialist and Republican elements, who had their own goals – a socialist Republic of Ireland. A march planned from Belfast to Derry turned into utter chaos as Loyalists attacked the participants, who got no protection from the police – on the contrary, they were seen and filmed joining in the attacks on the marchers. In Derry, policemen smashed their way into a supermarket and attacked shoppers; in the Bogside policemen rioted in the streets smashing windows and attacking anyone foolish enough to be out. All of this

in 1778 but was taken down again in 1801 because it was about to fall down, and the spire you see before you was put in its place. The interior is impressive, and has great wooden pews, those at the back very usefully allowing people to rest their heads while listening to interminable sermons. The regular pew ends are all

! St Columb's Cathedral is the first post-Reformation church to have been built in the British Isles.

fuelled the Free Derry movement: its slogan appeared on the gable end of a block of houses; moderates left the movement and it became dominated by Republicans. Support for the IRA, which had been practically defunct, increased.

The Battle of the Bogside began in August 1969, when fighting broke out between the Loyalist Apprentice Boy marchers and Catholics from the Bogside. The battle raged for two days, and CS gas was fired into the Bogside. The Taoiseach, Jack Lynch, called for the UN to enter what was effectively an out-of-control situation. Finally British troops entered the city, replacing the RUC. But three years later worse was to come: in January 1972 a civil rights march was fired on by paratroopers, killing 13, many by shots to the back. Another person died later of his wounds. The event came to be known as Bloody Sunday.

During this time parts of the city had become no-go areas for the army. After a series of IRA bombs in Belfast and Derry the British Prime Minister, James Callaghan, gave the order to clear the no-go areas, and Operation Motorman began. Tanks and armoured cars were brought into the city as the biggest British military operation since Suez began in the Bogside and in Protestant no-go areas.

individually carved, and the Gothic roof arches rest on the carved heads of past bishops.

The church also houses some crumbling flags, one of which is a pre-St Patrick's cross Union Jack. The yellow flags are replacements for Bastille flags taken from the besieging French troops of 1689; they ought to be white, but when the replacements were made, the originals had turned yellow with age and that yellow was taken for the correct colour. The other flags were donated by American battalions stationed in Derry during the war. There is a silver cross made of roof nails from the ruins of Coventry cathedral. The Chapter House is a treasure of junk – a chair said to be made from the pear tree that Robert Lundy climbed when he escaped from the besieged city, huge padlocks used to lock the gates of the city, gold pieces given by William to his loyal supporters and a doctored photo of Cecil Frances Alexander (see above) – if you look closely you will see that only the face and shoulders are a photo and the body has been painted in. In the lobby is the cannonball that carried the message telling those inside to surrender.

## St Columba's Church

Off Bishop St, **T** 7126 2301. *Open summer, 0900-2100; winter, 0900-2030.*

Back up on the walls, the double-bastioned west side looks out over some waste ground and beyond to St Columba's Church, which stands on the site of Tempull Mor (the medieval cathedral). It is possible to walk down to the church through Bishop's Gate, passing the barricaded Fountains Estate on the left, and turning right at the lights at Barrack Street. The church now standing dates back to 1784, very early in the Catholic church-building era. Inside are vast quantities of Connemara marble, and banks upon banks of fluorescent lights and candles, more reminiscent of a Buddhist temple than a Catholic church.

## Bogside
*Map 5, C/D 1/2, p253*

As the walls go on, past **'Roaring Meg'**, the cannon dedicated by the London Fishmongers, the view becomes the Bogside, and beyond it the Creggan estate. Below, out of sight, tucked in behind the wall, is the monument to those who died on Bloody Sunday. To the right is the **Free Derry mural** and beyond all the newly erected

## The Bogside Murals

The murals on the walls around the Free Derry mural depict key moments in the Troubles and they are the work of three local artists – Tom Kelly, Kevin Hasson and William Kelly – who lived through the conflict. "The story of the Bogside is our story and vice versa. Our murals stand therefore as the not-too-silent witnesses to the colossal price paid in suffering and brutalisation by hopelessly innocent people in their struggle for basic human rights. Our fervent wish is that the peace process will give us time to put right what has been so drastically put wrong."

The mural of a young girl is that of 14-year-old Annette McGavigan, the 100th victim and the first child to die in the conflict. The mural of Bernadette Devlin, a leader of the civil rights movement who was elected to the British parliament, pays homage to the many women who took part in the struggle for civil rights. The banging of dustbin lids, in the background, was a familiar tactic used to alert Bogsiders to the fact that the British army was in the neighbourhood. The grey and white mural of a petrol bomber was painted in 1994 to mark the 25th anniversary of the Battle of the Bogside.

A book of the murals, *Murals*, is available from the **Bookworm** bookshop in Bishop St, **T** 7128 2727, the Eason bookstore in the Foyleside Shopping Centre, or through the website www.bogsideartists.com.

and already crumbling council houses is **St Eugene's** Roman Catholic Cathedral (**T** 7126 2894) designed by several hands, the last of which was Liam McCormack, creator of the altar in Armagh.

Behind you, inside the city walls, is the **Apprentice Boys' Hall**, built in 1937. On the walls overlooking the Bogside once stood a 27-m tall monument to George Walker, successor to Lundy and governor of Derry at the time of the siege. It was blown up in 1973, and the head changed hands several times. It was beside this statue that the effigy of Lundy was traditionally burned in December, but in recent times, out of respect for their Bogside neighbours, the Apprentice Boys now burn it outside the walls on the south side in the Fountains area.

Continuing along the city wall, you pass the **First Derry Presbyterian Church**, originally built in 1690, rebuilt during the Georgian period and added to in 1863. What you see is almost entirely of Victorian construction with sandstone Corinthian pillars. This was one of the first places of worship not affiliated to the Church of Ireland that was allowed within the city walls.

## Tower Museum

Union Hall Pl, **T** 7137 2411. *Sep-Jun, Tue-Sat and Bank Holiday Mon, 1000-1700, last admission 1630; Jul-Aug, Mon-Sat, 1000-1700, last admission 1630. £4.  Map 5, C4, p253*

At Magazine Gate in the north corner of the walled city, this is a modern recreation of an ancient tower house that once stood here. The museum has won many awards, and deservedly so: it's the only museum in Ireland that makes any effort at all to confront the events of the last 30 years with anything near objectivity. What's more, it's interesting, relaxing and provides an excellent balance between information and artefacts. Towards the end of the trip around the museum you enter a mock-up street with orange, white and green kerbstones on one side, and red, white and blue stripes on the other. Above the kerbstones, display cases give two versions of the events of the last century. A permanent Armada in

! One exhibit you won't see in the Tower Museum is the AK47
• machine gun contributed by the IRA, which was confiscated
by the police.

Ireland exhibition is about to open and this should make a visit here even more irresistible.

● *The exit from the museum brings you into the Craft Village. Out of the summer months this really doesn't shine as a place to visit, but in summer the cafés, shops and open areas, where there is often live music and set dancing, are well worth a visit.*

## Guildhall

**T** *7137 7335. Mon-Fri, 0830-1700. Enquire at the tourist office regarding its reopening to the public. Map 5, C4, p253*

Leaving the walled city by Magazine Gate brings you to this Gothic extravaganza built in 1887 and burned down three times, once in 1908 by accident when only the main outer walls were left standing and the second and third times in 1972 by design, when the entire interior was wrecked. One of those convicted of the bombings in 1972 later sat as a council member in the same building. The interior is Victorian bombast, with vast stained glass windows representing the London liveries and the stories associated with Derry. Upstairs in the little kitchen alongside the great hall, look at the feet of George V in the stained-glass window portraying his coronation: he has his shoes on the wrong feet. In the Great Hall most of Brian Friel's plays were premiered. In the lobby is a stained-glass panel representing those who lost their lives on Bloody Sunday with, intriguingly, a sled with 'Rosebud' written on it. The statue of Queen Victoria has several fingers missing from the time when she was toppled over in one of the 1972 blasts.

### Amelia Earhart Centre

Ballyarnett, **T** 7135 4040. *Open Mon-Thu, 0900-1600, Fri 0900-1300. Free. Bus number D17 from the bus station.*

Five kilometres northwest of Derry is the Amelia Earhart Centre, commemorating the spot where she accidentally landed in 1932 having just made the first female solo crossing of the Atlantic. She mistook the village of Ballyarnett for Paris and landed there instead. Includes photos and memorabilia.

# Inishowen Peninsula, Donegal

*The Inishowen Peninsula of County Donegal in the Republic reaches out into the north Atlantic and a more extreme and isolated spot is hard to find in the British Isles. At its furthermost point it becomes the Malin Head, Ireland's most northerly point while to its east and west it is bounded by huge loughs. Setting all other considerations aside there is something enticing and irresistible about simply reaching this extremity of land. The pleasure which accompanies this achievement lies in the lyrical desolation of the peninsula's landscapes. Driving around here conveys more about what life must have been like for the peasant farmers of Ireland than any heritage centre can. The mountain scenery, and ancient sites are good for the soul. Better for the children stuck in the back of your car are the lovely, sandy deserted beaches where they can run amok and no one will hear them scream. Plus, once you are away from Buncrana, you will experience, probably for the first time in Ireland, the exhilarating absence of mass tourism. The area is often visited on speedy four-wheeled trips but as a place where people linger it is probably one of Ireland's least-known peninsulas and worth a few nights' stay to do it justice.*
▸▸ *See Sleeping p126, Eating p151, Pubs, bars and clubs p166*

**!** International direct dialling to the Republic of Ireland: 00353. Local Inishowen Peninsula area code: (0)74.

*Busways, T074-9382619, run Mon-Sat buses connecting Culdaff and Derry via Malin and Carndonagh. Mon-Sat buses also connect Greencastle and Derry via Moville and a third service connects Moville and Buncrana via Culdaff, Malin and Ballyliffin. Lough Swilly, T 074-9122863, T 048-71262017 (office in Derry), has daily buses between Derry and Moville and, on Mon, Wed, Fri and Sat, a Derry-Malin Head bus via Carndonagh.*

*Lough Swilly and Lough Foyle Ferry, T 074-9381901. The Lough Foyle service connects Greencastle with Magilligan in County Derry and operates a continuous shuttle service all year, Apr-Sep 0720-2150 (0900 Sun), Oct-Mar 0720-1950 (0900 Sun), costing €2 (£1.40) single, for foot passengers/cars and €3.50 (£2.40) return. Pay in euro or sterling. There are buses from Moville around the Peninsula, Mon-Fri, departing at 0730, 0905, 1145, and on Sat at 0905 and 1145.*

#  Sights

### Grianán of Aileach
*Map 6, C1, p254*

Grianán of Aileach is a stone fort strategically placed overlooking the flat land that separates the Inishowen Peninsula from the rest of the county. Built during the early Christian period, it was the headquarters of the O'Neill clan who ruled from here for centuries until a revengeful king of Munster attacked in 1101 and, so the story goes, ordered his men each to take away a stone from the walls. What you see today is largely a 19th-century reconstruction but managed more sensitively than many similar sites in the Republic.

There is no charge to visit the stone fort, unlike the nearby Grianán of Aileach Visitor Centre, on the main road where you turn off for the fort, which offers a fairly uninspiring exhibition on the top floor devoted to the fort's history.

**Burt Church**, the modern functioning church that stands on the corner before turning uphill for the stone fort, was designed in the mid-1960s by the same team of architects that produced St Michael's church at Cresslough. Like much of the best of modern Irish church architecture, St Michael's comes from the practise of Liam McCormick and partners. Cresslough is a curved shape which fits into the mountain backdrop, using ideas thought up by Le Corbusier in the 1950s such as spouting gargoyles and irregular coloured glass windows. This church, with its curving copper roof and sharp spire, echoes these ideas as well as looking towards the shapes of the stone fort.

## Fahan and Buncrana
*Map 6, C1, p254*

There are three reasons to stop in the village of Fahan: a modest but good beach, superb food for an evening meal that outclasses anything Buncrana can offer and a cross-slab near the modern church that dates from around the eighth century, decorated with elegant Latin crosses and carrying a barely decipherable but unique Greek inscription from early Christian Ireland.

There is very little reason to stop in Buncrana, even though this is the main town and resort on the peninsula. The beach (5 km long) attracts crowds of Irish holidaymakers during the summer but you can escape the hustle and bustle by seeking out the small beach that is reached by a path from the pier at the north end of the long main street.

## Buncrana to Ballyliffin
*Map 6, A/B1, p254*

An alternative to the direct inland route to Carndonagh from Buncrana involves taking the R238 road north and following signs for **Dunree Fort** (**T** 074-9361817, Jun-Sep, Mon-Sat 1000-1800,

Sun 1300-1800, €4) where there is a small military museum with displays on the fort's history, assorted weaponry and a tea-room. It is not very interesting, but the small sheltered **beach** has its charm and there are fabulous views of Lough Swilly across to Fanad Head.

Back on the main road the journey continues north up through the dramatic Mamore Gap before descending 243 m and bringing **Dunaff Head** and the bay into view.

● *The Rusty Nail is a fine old country pub that you pass on the road, serving food in the evenings during the summer and a popular Sunday lunch.*

Shortly after the pub a signposted turning off to the left leads to sandy **Tullagh Bay**, while the R238 continues on to the village of **Clonmany** where an angling festival takes place annually in August. A little way before entering the next village of Ballyliffin, on the main road, bicycles can be hired from *McEleney's Cycles*, **T** 074-9376541, and day trips made to nearby **Pollan Bay**, sandy but not safe for swimming, where you could have a picnic and visit **Doagh Famine Village** (**T** 074-9378078, Easter to Sep, 1000-1730, €5), the visitor centre focuses on the impact of the Famine.

## Around Carndonagh
*Map 6, B2, p254*

The alternative inland route to Carndonagh is by way of the R238 to Drumfree and then the R244. It is the quickest way to reach Malin Head from Buncrana and takes you across flat and lonely countryside where turf is still cut. Carndonagh is an undistinguished small town but a useful watering hole and home to the last supermarket south before Malin Head.

One reason to stay hereabouts for a night or two might be the surprising number of early Christian sites in the vicinity (ask at the helpful tourist office, see p29, for more details). Entering the village from Ballyliffin you will have already have passed **Donagh Church**, where there is a group of early Christian monuments made up of a cross and two carved stones from around the ninth century, while to the east of town there are the **Carrowmore high crosses** and the **Clonca Church cross**. They are not visually arresting and will prove disappointing if you are expecting something along the lines of Clonmacnoise; but some archaeologists think they may be the result of some independent missionary movement from Scotland.

### Malin and Malin Head
*www.malinhead.ie. Map 6, A1/2, 254*

The R238 presses on to the village of Malin, situated where a charming 10-arch stone bridge crosses Trawbreaga Bay. The neat triangular village green bears testimony to its origins as a 17th-century planter's creation and the sparse tidiness of the place evokes a suitable sense of the terminal. North of the village a signposted detour leads to **Five Fingers Strand** and the oldest church (1784) still functioning on the peninsula. The beach is exhilarating to walk along but swimming is dangerous here.

Malin Head, marked by the remains of a 19th-century signal tower, lacks visual drama, so your imagination must get to work on the flat vista of surrounding grass that faces out to uninhabited Inishtrahull Island. You are standing on the most northerly piece of Irish mainland and the next stop north is Greenland. Weather reports, first recorded here in 1870, still feature in the Shipping Forecast and the buildings of the meteorological station can be seen at the head. Just east of the head, **The Cottage** has some photographs of historical interest and a path leads east past the Seaview Tavern to the **Wee House of Malin**, a hermit's rock cell in the cliff. Birdwatchers can listen for the elusive corncrake and in autumn time migrating gannets, shearwaters and skuas pass overhead.

## Culdaff

*Map 6, A2, p254*

The route south that avoids going back through Malin takes you through the small village of Culdaff before carrying on through fairly deserted countryside as far as Moville or by way of a narrow winding road to Stroove. But there is more to Culdaff than meets the eye. In late June every year the **Culdaff Sea Angling Festival** (**T** 074-9379141) attracts anglers from all over the country and overseas for cash prizes, cups and trophies.

In early October the **Charles Macklin Autumn School** is an arts festival (**T** 074-9379104, 074-9397427, www.charlesmacklin.com) based around the life of the actor and playwright Charles Macklin (1697-1797). The festival lasts over three days of a weekend and includes drama, storytelling, the ancient Irish tradition of recitation, music sessions, creative writing workshops, art exhibitions and visiting writers.

● *While both these occasions bring seasonal life and laughter to Culdaff, there is also entertainment most of the time at the remarkable McGrory's pub (see pages 127, 153 and 166).*

**Bocan stone circle** lies to the south of Culdaff near Bocan church, but many of the stones have collapsed.

## Stroove to Muff

*Map 6, B3-C2, p254*

The lough-facing east side of the Inishowen Peninsula stretches from Stroove and Inishowen Head to the blink-and-it's-gone village of Muff barely inside the border with Northern Ireland. At Stroove there is a signposted walk, with fine views of Inishowen Head along the way, to picnic tables near a lighthouse, and you could walk from here to Kinnagoe Bay and return by the same route.

**Greencastle** is a fishing port at the mouth of Lough Foyle with the ruins of an ancient castle that are crumbling away on the coast and an early 19th-century fort, which is now a bar and restaurant (see p153). There is a fair choice of places to enjoy a meal, and infinitely better than what is available further down the coast in listless Moville.

The R238 hugs the coast all the way from Moville to the tiny village of **Muff**, where there is more going on than meets the eye. The place comes alive when the annual festival (**T** 074-9384024, 074-9384982, www.mcdco-op.com) is unleashed over the holiday weekend at the end of July. This is a family festival aimed chiefly at local people with activities for children during the daytime and music sessions in the evening. If you want to experience rural Ireland at its best this would be a good place to aim for during the long weekend.

Sleeping

107

In Dublin, hotel prices go up in summer and at weekends; but in Belfast for many years the opposite has happened. During the summer restaurants, guesthouses and  shops closed down for the marching season, and at weekends the city centre emptied, a throwback to the old days of car bombs and assassinations. Accommodation prices still reflect those days with prices dropping at weekends although with the advent of cheap flights from Britain things are beginning to change. There are no great bargains in the city centre but the hotels are classy enough. There are more modest places to the south of the city around the university, while B&Bs and hostels throughout the city provide cheaper accommodation. The guesthouses and B&Bs tend to cost around £40-60 for a double room, the higher end having en suite bathrooms in slightly bigger houses, the lower end being 1 or 2 rooms in someone's house with a shared bathroom. The most convenient of these are in the university area in the side streets between Malone and Lisburn roads. Eglantine Avenue has several good value places.

## ★ Sleeping price codes

| | | |
|---|---|---|
| **L** | over £165/€240 |
| **A** | £130/€190 -£165/€240 |
| **B** | £100/€140 -£130/€190 |
| **C** | £75/€110-£100/€140 |
| **D** | £55/€80 -£75/€110 |
| **E** | £35/€50-£55/€80 |
| **F** | £15-€20 -£35/€50 |
| **G** | less than £15/€20 |

The categories refer to the price of a double room.

# City centre

### Hotels

**L Radisson SAS**, 3 Cromac Pl, **T** 9043 4065, www.radissonsas.com. *Map 1, F6, p246* The latest addition to the posh hotels in the city. Pool, nice location, all the Radisson luxuries.

**L-A Malmaison Belfast**, 34-38 Victoria St, **T** 9022 0200, Belfast@ malmaison.com. *Map 4, D5, p252* This is the third incarnation of these beautiful old buildings that were once warehouses. In their new Malmaison style they hold a classy boutique hotel with 64 bespoke rooms, all black, cream and burgundy, with broadband, cable TV and DVD players. Generous freebie toiletries too.

**L-A TENsq**, 10 Donegall Sq East, **T** 9024 1001, www.tensquare.co.uk. *Map 4, G2, p252* Very classy boutique hotel in beautiful old bank buildings beside the City Hall. Deep colours and lots of attention to detail in the rooms means that this place fills up, especially at weekends. Has weekend break bargains but book early.

**A-B Europa Hotel**, Great Victoria St, **T** 9027 1066, www.hastingshotels.com. *Map 2, G7, p249* The best you can say about his rather ugly eastern-European looking building is that it's central and comfortable and that it stood here for years when the big hotel chains were nowhere to be seen.

**D Travelodge Belfast City**, 15 Brunswick St, **T** 0870-7522235. *Map 4, G1, p252* The best-value for the city centre, at £59.00 per room (which can sleep up to 4) without breakfast. Newly renovated but slightly cramped and characterless rooms. Also has restaurant.

**E Days Hotel**, 40 Hope St, **T** 9024 2494, **T** 0800-0280 400 (free phone), www.dayshotelbelfast.com. *Map 2, F7, p249* Another great bargain for families right in the city centre. Room rate of £69.99, lower at weekends with children staying free in parents' room.

### Hostels

**F Linen House Youth Hostel**, 18-29 Kent St, **T** 9058 6400, www.belfasthostel.com. *Map 2, D7, p249* Close to the main bus and train terminals, the main shopping area and City Hall, this is one of the largest of Belfast's hostels, in a renovated linen factory. Lots of room, large, well-equipped kitchen, good security. Mixed and single-sex dormitories. Double rooms. Left luggage room, bike storage, laundry, internet. Book in advance in the high season.

# Laganside

### Hotels

**L Belfast Hilton**, 4 Lanyon Pl, **T** 9027 7000, www.hilton.co.uk/belfast. *Map 2, F11, p249* Don't be put off by the dull reception

**★ Budget sleeping options**

- **Paddy's Palace**, p115.
- **Linen House Hostel**, p110
- **The Ark**, p115
- **Belfast International Hostel**, p115
- **Elms Village**, p114

and uniformed staff: if you can possibly afford it – stay here. It is a masterpiece of modernity in a sea of pompous Victoriana. Great views over the river, wonderful Hilton rooms, fluffy bathtowels, fitness centre and tiny pool, great *Sonoma* Restaurant with glass walls overlooking a hundred years of industry. Amazing discounts at weekends and serves up a good breakfast.

# Golden Mile and the University

## Hotels

**L-A Holiday Inn**, 22 Ormeau Av, **T** 0870-4009005, www.belfast. holiday-inn.com. *Map 2, H8, p249* Very central, comfortable rooms, leisure centre, close to the Golden Mile.

**B-C Crescent Townhouse**, 13 Lower Cres, **T** 9032 3349, www.crescenttownhouse.com. *Map 3, B7, p251* A small hotel with large, attractively appointed rooms. Set in the centre of the Golden Mile, its restaurant and bar are popular with office workers on their way home from work. The hotel itself is quiet, with the lobby upstairs, away from the activity of the bar and restaurant.

**C-D Duke's Hotel**, 65-67 University St, **T** 9023 6666, www.dukeshotelbelfast.com. *Map 3, D8, p251* Well located at the

> ### ▶ The Ulster Fry
>
> Sounds kind of scary doesn't it? As if you'd have to shout 'No surrender' before eating it, but it's worth a try in one of the really good B&Bs which haven't yet heard of, or care about, cholesterol overload. Basically the Ulster Fry is an extension of the 'full Irish' as they like to call it down south – bacon, sausage, mushrooms, black and white pudding, eggs, grilled tomatoes – with the addition of a little cake called fadge. This is made from cooked potatoes, milk and butter, mixed with plain flour and fried in little cakes, an Irish version of hash browns but much nicer.

end of the Golden Mile, interesting restaurant, big rooms, gym, good weekend rates.

**C-D Holiday Inn Express**, 106A University St, **T** 9031 1909, www.exhi-belfast.com. *Map 3, C9, p251* Excellent value hotel (rate includes breakfast) close to the Golden Mile. Also has a restaurant.

**C-D Wellington Park Hotel**, 21 Malone Rd, **T** 9038 5050, www.mooneyhotelgroup.com. *Map 3, E6, p250* Geared to business clientele, near to the Golden Mile, secure car parking. Largish, family-owned place which welcomes families, and has some good weekend break offers which bring it into a lower category.

**D Benedicts of Belfast**, 7-21 Bradbury Pl, Shaftesbury Sq, **T** 9059 1999, www.benedictshotel.co.uk. *Map 3, B7, p251* There's a very themed feel to this hotel with vaguely Gothic decor that uses reclaimed features from older buildings. It's also very central, has big rooms and is excellent value for money, especially at weekends if you don't mind late nights and a bit of noise. Restaurant and

Sleeping

breakfast to the sound of local music stations. Checking-in time 1400. 'Beat the clock' menu in the restaurant means the earlier you eat the less you pay.

**D Ivanhoe Hotel**, 556 Saintfield Rd, south along Ravenhill Rd, **T** 9081 2240, www.ivanhoeinn.co.uk. Small, family-run hotel in pleasant, rural surroundings with well-appointed big rooms, a comfortable bar that doubles as a bistro in the evenings and a more formal restaurant for dinner. Bus 84 from Howard St (east of Donegall Sq south) or taxi from the centre. Open for Sunday lunch.

**D Madison's**, 59-63 Botanic Av, **T** 9033 0040, www.madisonshotel.com. *Map 3, C7, p251* A very trendy and seriously design-led, modern hotel, popular with local swingers. Also has a restaurant which fills up most nights. Could get noisy at weekends when the club and bar get busy so only stay here if you are a night bird.

---

### Guest houses and B&Bs

**D Ravenhill House**, 690 Ravenhill Rd, **T** 9020 7444, www.ravenhillhouse.com. *Map 1, H5 (off), p246* Pretty, child-friendly Victorian house in quiet location off the Ormeau Rd. Open fires, library, lots of maps and information. Offers a good breakfast (including vegetarian option).

**D Tara Lodge**, 36 Cromwell Rd, **T** 9059 0900, www.taralodge.com. *Map 3, B8, p251* Close to Botanic Avenue with all its bars and restaurants and walking distance from the centre. Good transport links, tasty breakfasts, private car park but lots of noise from the train station right behind the building. Ask for a room at the front.

**E All Seasons B&B**, 356 Lisburn Rd, **T** 9068 2814, allseasons@fsmail.net. *Map 3, E4, p250* Another small, well-placed house, albeit set on the main Lisburn Rd, with off-street parking and friendly service.

**E Avenue House**, 23 Eglantine Av, **T** 9066 5904, stephen.kelly6@ntlworld.com. *Map 3, E5, p250* A Victorian-style B&B. Rooms have en suite bathrooms and there's private parking available.

**E Eglantine Guest House**, 21 Eglantine Av, **T** 9066 7585. *Map 3, E5, p250* Inexpensive for a guesthouse. The same rates and facilities are also available at **E Liserin Guest House**, 17 Eglantine Av, **T** 9066 0769. *Map 3, E5, p250*

**E Helga Lodge**, 7-13 Cromwell Rd, **T** 9032 4820. *Map 3, C8, p251* Right in the heart of the Golden Mile on the corner of Botanic Avenue, this large rambling B&B is particularly good value but most rooms do not have en suite facilities.

**E Marine Guest House**, 30 Eglantine Av, **T** 9066 2828, www.marineguesthouse3star.com. *Map 3, E4, p250* Another well located, good value place close to the restaurants of Lisburn Rd and within walking distance of town (good buses into the centre too). Off-street parking.

### Halls of residence and hostels

**E Elms Village**, 78 Malone Rd, **T** 9038 1608, qehor@qub.ac.uk. *Map 3, E6, p250* Hall of Residence with single and twin rooms available during vacation periods, 24 Dec-7 Jan, 7-21 Apr, 19 Jun-10 Sep. Kitchen, TV room, laundry. Public phones.

**E Farset International Hostel**, 466 Springfield Rd, **T** 9089 9833, www.farsetinternational.com. *Map 1, F1, p246* Out of town and set in scenic countryside, this is an upmarket place with restaurant as well as self-catering facilities.

F **The Ark**, 18 University St, **T** 9032 9626, www.arkhostel.com. *Map 3, C7, p251* Hostel comprising two Georgian townhouses, with two kitchens and both double and single rooms.

F **Belfast International Hostel**, 22 Donegall Rd, **T** 9032 4733, www.hini.org.uk. *Map 3, B6, p250* This is a very central hostel, right in the heart of the best nightlife in the city. Double and family rooms as well as dorm beds. Secure parking and internet access.

F **Paddy's Palace**, 68 Lisburn Rd, **T** 9033 3367, www.paddyspalace.com. *Map 3, C5, p250* Big new addition to the hostel scene in Belfast, this is one of a chain of hostels which aim to give you the Irish experience. Loads of offers for long term stays, reductions for staying at other Paddy's Palaces, breakfast included in rate, free internet.

F-G **Arnie's Backpackers**, 63 Fitzwilliam St, **T** 9024 2867, www.arniesbackpackers.co.uk. *Map 3, C6, p250* Dorm beds only, self-catering hostel in a small Victorian house off the Golden Mile.

Sleeping

## Self-catering

Most self-catering accommodation in the city is centred around the university area. Units can be hired for a week or a weekend and accommodate between 2 and 6 people. Some work out at the range of a budget hotel for 6 people and much less for larger parties while others charge per person and can be relatively expensive.

B-D **Belfast City Apartments**, c/o Greer Park Av, **T** 9064 9996, www.belfastcityapartments.co.uk. A range of places sleeping up to 4 people in modern apartment block. Lots of home comforts.

**B-D City Resorts**, 361 Lisburn Rd, **T** 0700-2935244, www.cityresorts.com. A range of apartments in various locations around the city to suit all sizes of parties. Check out the website for what is available.

**C Malone Grove Apartments**, 60 Eglantine Av, **T** 9038 8000, www.malonelodgehotel.com. *Map 3, E5, p250*  1- to 2-bedroom apartments near university. Price includes housekeeping and breakfast. Rate is per person sharing.

**D Belfast Town Homes**, Ardenlee Green, Ravenhill Rd, **T** 9080 6116, www.belfasttownhomes.co.uk. 2- to 3-bedroom apartments (sleeping 2-6) in south Belfast. Rate is per apartment so cheaper for larger groups.

## East of the city

**C Rayanne House**, 60 Demesne Rd, Holywood, **T** 9042 5859. *Map 1, A12, p247*  Holywood is a middle-class neighbourhood a short way east of Belfast City Airport, with its own cluster of restaurants and this decidedly superior guest house in a large, detached and quiet house. The Victorian/Edwardian decor is something you'll either love or loathe, but the whole house exudes comfort and calm. Dinner can be arranged in advance but there are lots of local eateries.

## County Down

### Downpatrick

**C Tyrella House**, 100 Clanmaghery Rd, **T** 4485 1422, www.hiddenireland.com/tyrella. A good choice for an out-of-town, country house sort of stay, has its own beech woods, private beach and stables. Also has a self-catering cottage.

**D Denvir's**, 14-16 English St, **T** 4461 2012. An ancient building recently renovated to a Spartan prettiness. The dining room has the most enormous fireplace with the old hooks that were used for smoking meat still in place. Huge rooms, very central but quiet. The best place to stay in Downpatrick. Single/double is £32.50/£55.

**E Arolsen**, 47 Roughal Park, **T** 4461 2656 bryancoburn@ compuserve.com. Fairly central B&B. Evening meals by arrangement. Single/double is £20/£36.

**E Dunnleath House**, 33 St Patrick's Dr, **T** 4461 3221. A B&B in Downpatrick with two big triple rooms.

**E-F Hillside**, 62 Scotch St, **T** 4461 3134. A B&B in a listed Georgian house with three double rooms, one with en suite bathroom and a Residents' lounge. Single/double £18/£35.

## Annalong

**B Glassdrumman Lodge**, 85 Mill Rd, signposted off the main road at the Newcastle end of the village, **T** 4376 8451, www.glassdrummanlodge.co.uk. Reassuringly peaceful atmosphere, quality accommodation and good food help make this a congenial place to stay for a night or two.

**E The Sycamores**, 52 Majors Hill, **T** 4376 8279. Old farmhouse building with parts dating back to the 18th century and views out to sea.

## Around Kilkeel

**E Heath Hall**, 160 Moyadd Rd, **T** 4176 2612. A friendly and comfy farmhouse B&B, about a mile inland, fine for a one-night stopover.

E **Mourne Abbey**, 16 Greencastle Rd, **T** 4176 2426. Half a mile south of town, this comfortable B&B opens from Easter-Sep and an evening meal is an option.

## Rostrevor

E **Fir Trees**, 16 Killowen Old Rd, Rostrevor, **T** 4173 8602, www.firtrees-bedbreakfast.co.uk. A bungalow B&B overlooking the lough.

## Newry

B **Canal Court Hotel**, Merchants Quay, **T** 3025 1234, www.canalcourthotel.com. Alex Ferguson stayed here and, while that might deter the anti-Man U league, he knew, as usual, what he was doing and chose the best on offer. Smart bedrooms and a leisure centre with pool.

D **Mourne Country Hotel**, 52 Belfast Rd, **T** 3026 7922, www.mournecountryhotel.com. A little way out of town at the roundabout on the Belfast Rd, with weekend and midweek deals.

E **Millvale House**, 8 Millvale Rd, **T** 3026 3789. B&B with four rooms, serves high tea for £5, dinner for £7 and stays open all year.

F **Carrow House**, 22 Newtown Rd, Belleeks, **T** 3087 8182. This B&B is not in town, but a double here only costs £24. Open Apr- Sep.

There are numerous other keenly-priced B&Bs in and around town: enquire at the tourist office.

### Self-catering in the Mourne Mountains

Self-catering accommodation is worth considering for an extended stay while walking the Mourne mountains.

**Lecale Cottages**, 125 Kilbroney Rd, Rostrevor, **T** 4173 8727, www.rostrevorholidays.com. Three self-catering, traditional-style cottages, overlooking the lough and costing £220-£270 a week. It is often possible to book a self-catering place for less than a week.

**Mountains of Mourne Cottages**, Hannas Close, Kilkeel, **T** 4176 5999, www.travel-Ireland.com/hannas. Restored traditional Irish cottages sleeping from two to six people and a four-person cottage in low/high season is £275/£375.

**Manx View**, 257 Kilkeel Rd, Annalong, **T** 4176 3222, margaret_bingham@hotmail.com. Sleeps 3, close to beach, £170-£225 depending on time of year.

**Mountain View House**, 20 Head Rd, Moyadd, Kilkeel, **T** 4172 3120, sjlavery@fsadvice.co.uk. Rural self-catering from £170-£250 a week.

## Dundalk and the Cooley Peninsula

### Dundalk

**B Ballymascanlon House Hotel**, out of Dundalk on the road to the Cooley peninsula, **T** 042-9371124, www.ballymascanlon.com. This is a grand Victorian edifice modernized with top-class sports facilities but hardly able to forget the past with the impressive Proleek Dolmen from around 3000 BC in its grounds; a good restaurant.

**C-D Derryhale Hotel**, Carrickmacross Rd, Dundalk, **T** 042-9335471, derryhale@eircom.net. A listed Victorian building within walking distance of town. See also Eating, p146.

**D Rosemount**, Dublin Rd, Dundalk, **T** 042-9335878. Just south of town off the N1, this is generally regarded as one of the best B&B establishments in the area.

**E Fáilte House**, Dublin Rd, Dundalk, **T** 042-9335152. A reliable B&B, on the corner with Long Avenue.

---

### Carlingford

**B Ghan House**, Carlingford, **T** 042-9373682, www.ghanhouse.com. An 18th-century house with walled grounds, forbiddingly expensive room rates and an excellent restaurant.

**B-C McKevitt's Village Hotel**, Market Sq, Carlingford, **T** 042-9373116, www.mckevittshotel.com. A welcoming place but busy in the summer.

**C-F Carlingford Adventure Centre and Holiday Hostel**, Tholsel St, Carlingford, **T** 042-9373100, info@carlingfordadventure.com. Over 30 dorm beds and a small number of private rooms edging into the E price range.

**D Beaufort House**, Ghan Rd, Carlingford, **T** 042-9373879, www.beauforthouse.net. By the water's edge, this guesthouse has hotel-standard rooms with views.

**E Grove House**, Grove Rd, Carlingford, **T** 042-9373494. One of the least expensive B&Bs in town.

# North Antrim Coast

## Portrush

B&B rates peak in Jul and Aug to £25 per person, dropping to around £15 at other times for rooms sharing bathroom facilities.

**B Magherabuoy House Hotel**, 41 Magherabuoy Rd, **T** 7082 3507, www.magherabuoy.co.uk. Outside the town with unrivalled views over the Atlantic Ocean.

**E Maddybenny Farm**, 18 Maddybenny Park, **T** 7082 3394, www.maddybenny.freeserve.co.uk. This may be out of town, but a more gregarious guesthouse would be hard to find and your enjoyment of a visit will be proportional to your appetite for a gargantuan breakfast (porridge with Drambuie and cream as an appetizer) that makes the usual B&B offering seem like child's play.

**E Windsor Guest House**, 67 Main St, **T** 7082 3793. A family-run period townhouse in the heart of town.

**E-F Atlantis**, 10 Ramore Av, **T** 7082 4583. A B&B not in a quiet part of town, but with the advantage of a kitchen available for snacks.

**F Macools Hostel**, 35 Causeway St, Portrush, **T** 7082 4845, www.portrush-hostel.com. Close to the bus and train station, even closer to the beach, comfortable and well-provisioned, including a dog called Guinness.

## Portrush to Giant's Causeway

**A-B Bushmills Inn**, 25 Main St, Bushmills, **T** 2073 2339, www.bushmillsinn.com. One of the best hotels in Ulster and a place you will remember; saying it has nooks and crannies hardly does justice to its geography (check out the hidden room), complete with turf fires and gas lamps. See also p148.

**D Craig Park**, 24 Carnbore Rd, Bushmills, **T** 2073 2496, www.craigpark.co.uk. Big country house set in 20 acres with lovely views over the mountains of Donegal and the hills of Antrim.

**E Ahimsa**, 243 Whitepark Rd, Bushmills, **T** 2073 1383. A traditional cottage specializing in vegetarian meals and using produce from its organic garden.

**F Mill Rest Hostel**, Bushmills, **T** 2073 1222, www.hini.org.uk. A new Hostelling International place with a range of smart rooms, bicycle store and walled garden.

## Around Giant's Causeway

**D Whitepark House**, Whitepark Rd, **T** 2073 1482, www.whiteparkhouse.com. With three rooms sharing bathroom facilities, this has been warmly recommended by readers. B&B is £60 for a double and the odd-looking place is hard to miss on the road between the Causeway and Ballintoy.

**D-E Causeway Hotel**, Causeway Rd, **T** 2073 1226, www.giants-causeway-hotel.com. A stay here should prove more satisfying now than it did to Thackeray in 1842: "It was impossible to feel comfortable in the place, and when the car wheels were heard, I jumped up with joy to take my departure and forget this awful shore, that wild, dismal, genteel inn."

F **Ballintoy House**, Main St, Ballintoy, **T** 2076 2317. The house carries the 1737 date of its building on its front wall and the B&B single/double rate is £20/£34.

F **Sheep Island View**, Main St, Ballintoy, **T** 2076 9391, www.sheepislandview.com. In the centre of the village by the bus stop, has a terrific kitchen, includes one double, camping space, meals available, guided walks can be arranged, and musical entertainment in the pub most nights.

F **Whitepark Bay Hostel**, 6 miles west of Ballycastle on the A2, **T** 2073 1745, www.hini.org.uk. It's hard to beat this place. A top-notch YHANI hostel overlooking White Park Bay with 6-bed and 4-bed rooms, and 4 superb double rooms with TV and tea- and coffee-making facilities, foreign exchange, a restaurant and bike hire. Buses stop 200 metres away.

## Ballycastle

D **Marine Hotel**, North St, **T** 2076 2222, www.marinehotel.net. Fairly standard hotel with restaurant and fitness centre.

E **Ammiroy House**, 24 Quay Rd, **T** 2076 2621. This place with two rooms in a family house is typical of the B&Bs along this road.

E **Beechwood**, 9 Beechwood Av, **T** 2076 3631, stay@beechwoods.f9.co.uk. Can be recommended for its quiet location and friendly welcome. The house has two double rooms sharing a bathroom, but best value has to be the two chalet-type rooms at the back with their own facilities including a fridge and sink. No avoiding the Ulster fry-up though.

F **Ballycastle Backpackers**, 4 North St, **T** 2076 3612. A small hostel, but with four private rooms from £20.

**F Castle Hostel**, 62 Quay Rd, **T** 2076 2337. Has 40 beds including three private rooms for £20. The preferred hostel for some travellers.

### Rathlin Island

**E The Manor House**, **T** 2076 3964. A large Georgian house by the harbour, open all year and run by the National Trust as a B&B establishment. A single is £24 (£28 en suite), a double is £50 (£54 en suite).

**E Rathlin Guest House**, The Quay, **T** 2076 3917. Open Apr-Sep and evening meals are available.

**F Soerneog View Hostel**, **T** 2076 3954. Overlooks Mill Bay and is a short walk from the harbour. Open all year but only 3 beds – one double and two twin rooms. Book ahead in summer. £8 per person.

# Derry

There is a fair range of accommodation in Derry, most of which should be booked in advance. The hotels are modern and well-equipped but a bit disappointing in terms of character and style. The tourist office (see p29) will book accommodation for you if you arrive in town with none organized.

**C-D Tower Hotel**, The Diamond, **T** 7137 1000, www.towerhotel derry.com. *Map 5, D3, p253* The style is international/contemporary but given its significant location (it's the only hotel inside the city walls) it's a disappointingly charmless place to stay.

**D-E Da Vinci's Hotel**, 15 Culmore Rd, **T** 7127 9111, www.davincishotel.com. Inconveniently located, 1 mile (1.6 km) north of the city centre, but good eating and drinking options and inexpensively-priced rooms are available. There are also Da Vinci apartments, advertised from £67, in College Place, Strand Road.

E **Aberfoyle**, 33 Aberfoyle Terr, Strand Rd, **T** 7128 3333, aberfoyle@ntlworld.com. A B&B 5 minutes from the city centre. Good tourist advice.

E **Arkle House**, 2, Coshquin Rd, **T** 7127 1156, www.derryhotel.co.uk. A Victorian house offering B&B, 1½ miles northwest of the centre of Derry.

E **City of Derry Travelodge**, **T** 1800-709709, 0870 191 1733, www.travelodge.ie. *Map 5, B3, p253* From £40 a room sleeping up to two adults and two children, or three adults. Functional but affordable accommodation in a rather noisy spot where several discos turn out late at night and the punters wait for taxis. Ask for a room at the back.

E **The Inn at the Cross**, 171 Glenshane Rd, 3 miles from town centre, **T** 7130 1480, innatthecross@virgin.net.uk. Out-of-town guesthouse that thinks it's a hotel with popular restaurant and bar.

E **The Merchant's House**, 16 Queen St, **T** 7126 9691, www.thesaddlershouse.com. *Map 5, A2, p253* Lovingly restored Georgian house. Great breakfasts, lots of good information, sitting area and library. One room has an en suite bathroom. The most central B&B in town and best value place for single rooms.

E **The Saddler's House**, 36 Great James St, **T** 7126 9691, www.thesaddlershouse.com. *Map 5, B2, p253* Equally lovingly restored Victorian townhouse. All rooms have en suite bathrooms, lots of information, and good, informal breakfasts. The best, most central B&B option in town after The Merchant's House.

E **Abbey**, 4 Abbey St, **T** 7127 9000, www.abbeyaccommodation. com. *Map 5, C2, p253* Five rooms, mostly with en suite bathrooms, in the Bogside, a 5-minute walk to city centre. A friendly B&B in a historic location.

E **Derry City Independent Hostel**, 44 Great James St, **T** 7137 7989; and F **Derry Backpackers**, 4 Asylum Rd, **T** 7137 7989, derryhostel@hotmail.com. *Map 5, B2, p253* Both hostels, under same ownership, charge £10 for a single and £14 for a private room, including breakfast and internet access. The one on Great James St has the larger rooms but no private doubles whereas there are some private rooms in Asylum St. Newly acquired houses in Princess St will increase the number of beds and more double rooms will be available.

F **Paddy's Palace**, 1 Woodleigh Terr, Asylum Rd, **T** 7130 9051, www.paddyspalace.com. *Map 5, A2, p253* This hostel is linked with the company that runs small group tours around Ireland (www.paddywagontours.com) so expect gaggles of travellers but it also functions as a walk-in hostel. All beds are in dorms, £10 per person including breakfast, and there is a kitchen.

# Inishowen Peninsula, Donegal

### Fahan and Buncrana

A-C **St John's Country House and Restaurant**, at the Buncrana end of Fahan, **T** 074-9360289. By the shores of Lough Swilly this place offers comfortable accommodation (with an exemplary breakfast) and a delightful dinner experience (see p151).

! International direct dialling to the Republic of Ireland: 00353. Local Inishowen Peninsula area code: (0)74.

## Carndonagh

**E Ashdale Farmhouse**, Malin Rd, **T** 074-9374017, www.ashdalehouse@eircom.net. A two-storey farmhouse on the road to Malin.

## Malin and Malin Head

**C-D Malin Hotel**, Malin Village, **T** 074-9370645, malinhotel@eircom.net. Faces the village green and is distinctively coloured both inside and out.

**F Malin Head Hostel**, Malin Head, 2 miles (3 km) from the headland, on the left side of the road, **T** 074-9370309. Open from Mar to Oct. Tidy, clean and efficient and bike hire available.

**G Sandrock Holiday Hostel**, Port Ronan Pier, Malin Head, **T** 074-9370289, sandrockhostel@eircom.net. Open all year, has a laundry, bikes for hire and suggested walking routes. No private rooms.

## Culdaff

**D McGrory's**, **T** 074-9379104. Ten bedrooms with their own en suite bathroom facilities. See also pages 153 and 166.

**E Ceecliff House**, **T** 074-9379159. Does B&B in a modern house for around €30 per person.

## Stroove to Muff

**E Admiralty House**, Moville, **T** 074-9382529. Overlooking Lough Foyle and a 5-minute walk from Moville but only open Jun-Aug.

**E Bruach An Domhain**, T 074-9367359. Open Apr-Oct for B&B in a restored coastguard station overlooking Tremone Bay.

**E Dunroman**, Carrownaffe, Moville, T 074-9382234. Also overlooking Lough Foyle but open all year and set in a quiet cul-de-sac.

## Self-catering on Inishowen

**Marian Doherty**, Malin, T 074-9379294. Four-bedroom bungalow, 6 km from Main and 4 km from beach. From €60 nightly to €400 in July and August, available all year.

**River House**, Moville, T 074-9382052, hknorris@hotmail.com. Sleeps from seven to 10 from €375 to €550 in three houses set in private woodlands.

**Sheila Mailey**, Fanad, T 074-9121646. Sleeps up to four in two-bedroomed little house with sea view. From €150 midweek to €280 in summer.

Eating out in Northern Ireland is fun – it is affordable, if you choose well, and the Dublin problem of style taking precedence over good cooking wouldn't go down well here. Like the rest of us, Belfast has fallen in love with Asian food, and so modern Indian, Thai and Chinese eateries are a good option in the city. Pricey but challenging are the very trendy modern Irish restaurants, especially those that have a TV chef's name attached. They offer a nice mix of traditional Irish food with a special modern twist. Outside of Belfast there are little oases of good eating – Derry has one or two good places, while reliable, if less exciting, pub grub is on offer everywhere. Bear in mind, however, that out of the big centres lots of restaurants close or have very limited menus, particularly during the winter. Belfast has not yet embraced the vegetarian lifestyle but fear not, Asian places usually have several vegetarian options and most other restaurants offer at least one vegetarian dish; happily, veggie lasagne is a thing of the past.

## Eating price codes

**Prices**

₸₸₸ Expensive (over £30)
₸₸ Mid-range (£20-30)
₸ Cheap (less than £20)

The categories refer to the price of a 3-course meal, excluding drinks or tips.

### Some useful food and eating websites

**www.nifda.co.uk**, the Taste of Ulster website.
**www.foodstuffireland.com**, lots of information on Irish food and cooking.
**www.Irish-cookery-school.com**, Belle Isle Cookery School.

# City centre

Where once only used fast-food cartons whirled around the deserted windy streets of the city centre every evening, the inner city has again become a place for people to step out after the shops have closed. Several good restaurants have recently added to the good reasons for being in Belfast. With the development of the Odyssey Centre and the classy apartment blocks beside the river, new life is springing up around The Lagan Lookout area of the city and around the Waterfront Hall too.

## Restaurants

₸₸₸ **James Street South**, 21 James St South, **T** 9043 4310. *Map 2, G7, p249* Elegantly designed and serving accessible haute cuisine. Another place for a special night out. If you can't afford the evening menu, lunch is a bit cheaper.

¶¶¶ **Porcelain**, 10 Donegall Sq Sth, **T** 9024 1001. *Map 2, G8, p249* In the TenSquare Hotel, this place is much more than a typical hotel restaurant. It has an excellent reputation, is small and cosy and is often booked up long in advance at weekends. The cuisine is a kind of nouvelle-Irish-French with kedgeree, lamb Provençale, and some imaginative desserts.

¶¶¶ **Restaurant Michael Deane's**, 38 Howard St, **T** 9056 0000. *Map 2, G7, p249* The place to be seen in the city centre. Reservations well in advance are necessary as well as a well endowed credit card. Interestingly decorated with a *fin de siècle* mood to the dining room, big silver lids on the dishes and little brushes for the crumbs between courses. Great for a special occasion.

¶¶¶ **Roscoff Brasserie**, 7-11 Linenhall St, **T** 9031 1150. *Map 2, G8, p249* TV chef Paul Rankin's newest effort. French brasserie cuisine, white tablecloths, sophisticated and efficient atmosphere, masterly food. Set dinner won't put you too far into debt while a two course set lunch is moderately priced.

¶¶¶ **Sonoma**, in the Hilton hotel, Lanyon Pl, **T** 9027 7000. *Map 2, F11, p249* Best place of all in this area for the food and the views. It has a huge window looking out on to the river, extending the length of the room, and excellent modern Irish cuisine and lots of careful service. Pre-theatre menu comes into a lower price range.

¶¶ **Bank Gallery Restaurant**, The Edge, May's Meadow, **T** 9032 2000. *Map 2, G12, p249* An excellent pre-theatre menu of some good standard dishes such as salmon with saffron mash, confit duck with champ and chili jam or rib eye steak.

¶¶ **Bar Seven**, Odyssey Pavilion, **T** 9046 7070. *Map 2, C12, p249* One of the city's many trendy designer bars but its food stands out among the rest with a set dinner menu under £20 and

## Eating Irish

The traditional food of Northern Ireland is essentially home cooking, based on what the land and the sea can provide, and there are still traditional Irish dishes which are well worth looking out for. **Irish stew** is worth a try but you should also look out for Irish breads. There is **soda bread**, made with wheat flour and leavened with baking soda, and **soda farls**, a cross between a pancake and a roll made with white flour and again leavened with soda. Look too for **barmbrack**, more of a cake than a bread, traditionally produced at Hallowe'en and filled with little tokens which promise to tell the fortune of the family tucking into them. **Ulster scones** are made with potato, apples, flour, butter and eggs and baked in an oven.

There isn't room to describe all the things Irish people do with potatoes but look out for **boxty**, a mixture of flour and potatoes and buttermilk fried into little cakes and served nowadays filled with meat. My personal favourite is **champ** – perfect comfort food – mashed potatoes mixed with cooked scallions (spring onions) and served in a bowl with melted butter. Another Hallowe'en speciality is **colcannon**, similar to champ but more substantial with cabbage and leeks in the mix. Almost lost now, but still found occasionally, is **stampy**, a mixture of flour and grated potatoes cooked in the bastible pot over the open fire and smothered in butter.

Lastly, what list of Irish delicacies would be complete without a mention of that most traditional of workaday meals – **bacon and cabbage**. Even within my memory a country family would keep a pig and have it slaughtered and salted and kept for the winter. A joint would then be pulled out and cooked in a pot with cabbage and the two basic ingredients left to infuse one another's essential qualities. Serve with boiled potatoes still in their skins and mustard sauce. Yummy.

★ **Cheap eats**

**Best**

- **Chokdee**, p134
- **Irene and Nan's** evening specials, p135
- **La Tasca**, p136
- **Benedict's** Beat the Clock, p139
- **Maggie May's**, p143

some good offers on combined cinema tickets and dinner. Style is modern Irish and the place gets booked up well in advance.

🍴 **Chokdee**, 44 Bedford St, **T** 9024 8800. *Map 2, G8, p249* Open for lunch and dinner Mon to Sat. A Michael Deane offshoot serving a very original blend of southeast Asian, spicy stir fries and Italian home cooking. A good place to drop in on the spur of the moment. Lively and right at the bottom of this price range.

🍴 **Deane's**, 34-40 Howard St, **T** 9056 0000. *Map 2, G8, p249* Downstairs is a brasserie which is enormously popular, focusing on modern Irish cooking where dinner will cost £18 plus.

🍴 **Indian Ocean**, Odyssey Pavillion, **T** 9046 6888. *Map 2, C12, p249* A pretty standard but likeable Indian place with good vegetarian options, a children's menu and some western dishes.

🍴 **McHugh's**, close to the Albert Tower in Queen's Sq, **T** 9050 9999. *Map 2, D10, p249* A renovated 18th-century pub with an Asian fusion restaurant and bar food. Worth a visit for the interior of the pub alone.

🍴 **Oxford Exchange**, St George's Market, May St, **T** 9024 0014. *Map 2, G10, p249* This place is developing a good reputation as a hearty, meaty grill room with some curious versions of bangers

★ **Best**

**Vegetarian meals**

- **Beatrice Kennedy**, p140
- **Gingeroot**, p140
- **Indie Spice**, p140
- **Café Zinc**, p142
- **Archana**, p142

and mash, fish and chips as well as boar. All served with posh chips and grilled vegetable. Closed Sun.

🍴 **Red Panda**, 60 Great Victoria St, **T** 9046 6644. *Map 2, H7, p249* A good, Belfast-influenced, brightly lit Chinese place serving hot spicy Sichuan food alongside Belfast gravy and chips and more experimental offerings such as king prawns cooked in filo pastry.

🍴 **Tedford's**, 5 Donegall Quay, **T** 9043 4000. *Map 2, E10, p249* A well-established fish restaurant with the regulation Asian overtones in what was once an old ship's chandler shop. Good pre-theatre menu Tue-Sat makes for an affordable, comfortable meal close to the Waterfront.

🍴 **The Waterfront Brasserie**, Waterfront Hall, **T** 9024 4966. *Map 2, F10, p249* Does breakfasts and lunches, and dinner between 1800-1930 when there is a show on. Worth visiting for its views alone. Book in advance.

🍴 **Irene and Nan's**, 12 Brunswick St, **T** 9023 9123. *Map 2, H7, p249* A very trendy café/bar at night but during the day and early evening offers some great food. Try the early evening two or three course set menus which barely get up into double figures plus laughably inexpensive wine list.

¶ **La Tasca**, Odyssey Pavilion, **T** 9073 8241.  *Map 2, C12, p249*  A rather ordinary chain tapas bar/Spanish restaurant which comes into the inexpensive category.

¶ **Morning Star**, 17-19 Pottinger's Entry, **T** 9023 5986.  *Map 2, H7, p249*  No nonsense haute cuisine here – giant steaks, gravy dinners, and the occasional shark, kangaroo or crocodile for bushmeat lovers, followed by lashings of dessert.

¶ **Titanic Bar and Grill**, Odyssey Pavillion, **T** 9076 6990.  *Map 2, C12, p249*  A huge place cashing in on the Titanic connection with lots of memorabilia plastered over the walls, very down to earth grub – BBQ ribs, honey roast gammon, very edible desserts, a children's menu and respectable vegetarian options.

### Cafés and fast food

At lunchtime the city centre abounds with reasonably priced places for a designer sandwich or something more substantial. Several of them are open late on Thu till about 2100 for the late-night shopping.

**Bewleys**, Donegall Arcade.  *Map 2, E8, p249*  Branch of a chain which offers a little more than the traditional scones and tea.

**Café Paul Rankin**, 2 branches at 12-14 Arthur St and 27-29 Fountain St.  *Map 2, F9, p249*  Both are very popular, do big breakfast and lunch menus and are good for a long relaxed lunch till 1800 (2100 on Thu).

**Clements**, Donegall Sq West (and several other locations around the city centre).  *Map 2, F8, p249*  Good for lounging on the sofas, drinking coffee and munching sandwiches.

**Delaney's**, Donegall Arcade. *Map 2, E8, p249* Attractively designed with a wide, inexpensive menu, open Mon-Sat 0900-1700.

## Pub lunches

**Apartment**, right in the centre at Donegall Sq West, **T** 9050 9777. *Map 2, F8, p249* A cocktail bar with bar food, open daily till late.

**Fibber Magee's**, Keylan's Pl. *Map 2, G7, p249* Also does good food.

**White's Tavern**, Winecellar Entry. *Map 2, E8, p249* A more traditional menu, but the food has an excellent reputation and they do a roaring trade. Get there early.

# The Cathedral Quarter

Here too things are moving at a rate of knots with every once-derelict warehouse and burned-out building covered in scaffolding and designer hotels, bars and cafés rearing up out of the paving stones.

## Restaurants

¶¶ **Ba Soba**, 38 Hill St, **T** 9058 6868. *Map 2, D9, p249* Belfast's first noodle bar with lots of southeast Asian stir fries, Thai curries, noodle dishes and the atmosphere of a posh Bangkok bar. Lots of combination lunch and dinner options keeps prices low and there are early evening offers of less than £8 for a main course.

¶¶ **Duke of York**, Commercial Court. *Map 2, D9, p249* Very popular place serving slightly more than the usual pub grub.

¶ **The John Hewitt**, 51-53 Donegall St, **T** 9023 3768. *Map 2, D9, p249* A good place to check out, both for the pub food and for the traditional music and storytelling sessions.

¶ **Nichol Bar Brasserie**,12 Church Lane, caught between the city centre and the Cathedral Quarter, **T** 9027 9595. *Map 2, E9, p249* A tiny place serving Mediterranean-style food upstairs, lunch Mon-Sat, dinner Thu-Sat. Nicer in summer when the tables go out on the street and a Mediterranean atmosphere infuses more than just the menu.

¶ **Nick's Warehouse**, 35-39 Hill St, **T** 9043 9690. *Map 2, D9, p249* Serves thoughtful modern Irish cuisine in a vast old warehouse with an open kitchen and lots of bustle. Avoid weekends when it gets very busy and noisy. Lunch is very popular too. Closed Sun and Mon.

¶ **The Northern Whig**, 2 Bridge St, **T** 9050 9888. *Map 2, E9, p249* Really a designer bar with huge statues salvaged from eastern Europe but it has a better than average bar menu of pub standards, tandoori chicken, pasta, tapas and is very popular with the business fraternity at lunchtime.

## Golden Mile and the University

The Golden Mile really gets going in Dublin Road, and takes off along University Road and Botanic Avenue as far as University Street, extending a little into the side roads. At around £18 or less for an evening meal there are lots of good choices to make. Along Stranmillis Rd are several small, good places to eat, especially for lunch. In recent years the Lisburn Rd has also become a smart place for good things to eat, little delicatessens and neat clothing shops and is well worth making the effort of a trip out to some of the restaurants even if you are not staying in the area.

## Restaurants

¶¶¶ **Cayenne**, 7 Ascot House, Shaftsbury Sq, **T** 9033 1532.  *Map 3, B7, p251*  Starting at the *haute* end of the market, this is telly- chef Paul Rankin's well-established endeavour. Not a place for a romantic candlelight dinner, the place bustles from 1800 onwards, and the menu is about as eclectic as it can get. Sushi, Moroccan spiced lamb, Chorizo and borlotti beans, Italian penne, chicken with guacamole – just about every style of cuisine is mined here for its best and liveliest. Pleasant surroundings in a warm brown kind of way, service is just at the right pace. Open for lunch and dinner. Closed Sun. Reservations essential.

¶¶¶ **The Errigle Inn**, 312-320 Ormeau Rd, **T** 9064 1410.  *Map 1, H5, p246*  A labyrinth of bars whose Tom McGurran bar can claim a Michelin star for its gastropub style food. Ludicrously underpriced, dinner will set you back about £22 for three courses. While you are there check out the Oak Lounge still with its 1935 decor intact, a lovely mixture of elderly patrons who remember its opening and more bohemian types.

¶¶¶-¶¶ **Benedicts**, 7-21 Bradbury Pl, **T** 9059 1999.  *Map 3, B7, p251*  A heavily-designed restaurant and a dizzying range of menus which include several vegetarian options. Dinner in this Californian-influenced but fairly traditional restaurant will be around £20 plus. Lunch is around £8.50 for two courses. Prices for main courses are determined by the time you choose to eat: at 1900 any main course is £7, at 2000 it's £8 and so on. Carvery lunch on Sundays.

¶¶¶-¶¶ **Sun Kee**, Donegall Pass, opposite the heavily fortified police station, **T** 9031 2016.  *Map 3, B7, p251*  Reservations are essential at weekends and you still may have to queue. An excellent, authentic Chinese restaurant. While the majority of the dishes are

Eating

Eating

Cantonese there are lots of hotter Szechuan dishes and a few concessions to the blander western version of Chinese cooking. Like all good Chinese restaurants the eventual bill will depend on what you choose to eat and for the uninitiated they have a series of set banquets starting at about £22. If you can't get a table try the takeaway.

🍴 **Archana**, 53 Dublin Rd, **T** 9032 3719.  *Map 3, A7, p251*  Winner of lots of awards for its Indian food. Very respectable vegetarian lunch thalis for around £4. Dinner upstairs at around £15. Open Sun evenings.

🍴 **Beatrice Kennedy's**, 44 University Rd, **T** 9020 2290.  *Map 3, C7, p251*  Serving modern Irish cuisine this place offers a choice of early evening and dinner menus. The early evening menu is around £12 for two courses, while dinner works out around £26 plus. Open for lunch on Sun.

🍴 **Gingeroot**, 73-5 Gt Victoria St, **T** 9031 3124.  *Map 2, H7, p251*  Less authentic and much more trendy than Sun Kee (see above) this is a north Indian place with modern overtones and a huge plate glass window to sit beside. Lots of tandoor-cooked things and good breads. Try some of the north Indian desserts – too sweet for most western palates but very Indian.

🍴 **Indie Spice**, 159 Stranmillis Rd, **T** 9066 8100.  *Map 3, G7, p251*  A stylish modern place – no pictures of the Taj Mahal here. Lots of dishes, good for vegetarians and a takeout menu too.

🍴 **Istana Malaysian Restaurant**, 127 Gt Victoria St, **T** 9032 2311.  *Map 3, A7, p251*  Offers a brightly lit canteen-like atmosphere and a mixture of Malay, Chinese and Thai food. Particularly tasty is the Penang Laksa, all coconut and lemongrass. Open late Fri and Sat.

♔ **Lemongrass**, 1 University St, **T** 9032 4000. *Map 3, C7, p251* A branch of a popular chain of Asian fusion restaurants with a stylish modern interior and good lunch boxes to take out. Extra brownie points for being open daily, 1230-2300.

♔ **Madison's**, 59-63 Botanic Av, **T** 9050 9800. *Map 3, C7, p251* A popular restaurant, open daily, serving modern Irish/European cuisine and a more casual lunch menu.

♔ **The Maharajah**, 62 Botanic Av, **T** 9023 4200. *Map 3, C7, p251* Serves western versions of Indian cuisine, but good nonetheless.

♔ **Metro**, on the corner of Botanic Av and Lower Cres, **T** 9032 3349. *Map 3, B7, p251* A very stylish, modern place with Californian overtones, it has an inexpensive early evening menu (1800-1900). Very popular as a starting out point for Friday and Saturday night partyers.

♔ **Shu**, 253 Lisburn Rd, **T** 9038 1655. *Map 3, B7, p251* Closer to the city centre than Tatu this is a highly recommended minimalist, Asian-influenced place and very popular both for lunch and dinner. It's the kind of place for a whole evening out, with a cocktail bar in the basement to keep you there long after your meal is finished.

♔ **Tatu**, 701 Lisburn Rd, **T** 9038 0818. *Map 3, H2, p250* Definitely a bus ride away but worth the trip. It looks a little bit like a Soviet bus station outside and inside there is a huge barn-like bar at the front of the building and a more secluded, wood-panelled eating area at the back. In summer the chattering classes stand out on the deck sipping designer beers but food – Californian-inspired Irish – is served till 2145 most days after which it turns into a very trendy bar.

♔ **Villa Italia**, 37-41 University Rd, **T** 9032 8356. *Map 3, C8, p250* A long-established Italian joint, all chequered tablecloths, plastic grapevines and chianti bottles where long queues form for a table at weekends. Italian home cooking – pizzas, pasta and more. Open Sunday evenings.

---

## Cafés and fast food

If you are after fast food or a snack the area abounds with them. Bradbury Place probably has the largest range of big names, but there are plenty of other places worth a look.

♦♦♦ **Café Vincent**, 78 Botanic Av, **T** 9024 2020. *Map 3, C8, p251* Open daily. Does pasta dishes, snacks and designer coffees and is good for lunch.

♦♦♦ **Café Zinc**, 12 Stranmillis Rd, **T** 9068 2266. *Map 3, F7, p251* A little way beyond the Ulster Museum. In the evening the food is put away and it becomes a student-filled café/bar but through the day it serves an excellent menu of modern Irish cuisine, lots of fine cheeses and salads and more substantial dishes.

♦ **Giraffe**, 54 Stranmillis Rd, **T** 9050 9820. *Map 3, G7, p251* A slightly more interesting Clements clone with good, inexpensive food, sofas to lounge on and newspapers to read. Open till 2200 Mon-Sat and on Sunday mornings.

**Bishop's**, 32 Bradbury Pl. *Map 3, B7, p251* Good fish and chips.

**Clements**, 66 Botanic Av, T 9033 1827. *Map 3, B8, p251* A branch of this popular chain with leather sofas, big cups and speciality coffees. You'll be tempted to look around for Monica and Rachel. Good sandwiches, wraps, bagels and open on Sun mornings.

**Jenny's**, Dublin Rd. *Map 3, A7, p251* Country kitchenish and has a range of sandwiches, quiche and lasagne till 1700, 6 days a week.

**In the Crown**
*The perfect place to read the newspaper and get slowly sozzled.*

**Maggie May's**, Botanic Av. *Map 3, D7, p251* Has a vast inexpensive menu where vegetarians will feel as at home as Ulster fry and quiche lovers.

**Revelations Internet Café**, Shaftesbury Sq. *Map 3, B7, p251* Has, besides the World Wide Web, sandwiches and soup.

**Spuds**, Bradbury Pl. *Map 3, B7, p251* Looks awful but has a good menu of filled potatoes, and other fast things.

## Pub lunches

In the same area there are any number of pubs that do quite large lunch menus but which tend to focus on music and drink at night.

**Botanic Inn** and the **Eglantine**, both in Malone Rd.  *Map 3, F6, p250*  Both are student pubs but do pub food, the Botanic having the slightly better menu.

**The Globe**, University Rd.  *Map 3, C7, p251*  Does lots of meal deals including some with free pints. 1100-1800 except Sun.

**The King's Head**, 829 Lisburn Rd, **T** 9050 9950.  *Map 3, H1 (off map), p250*  A multiplex kind of a place with bar food as well as a posher restaurant upstairs. Later on in the evening you could check out the live music.

**Tapas Winebar**, 479 Lisburn Rd.  *Map 3, F3, p250*  Serves tapas in a convivial atmosphere on a first come first served basis. Closed Mon but open late for the rest of the week.

# County Down

### Downpatrick

♥♥♥ **Denvir's**, 14-16 English St, **T** 4461 2012. Hotel (see p117) with a restaurant which is enormously popular with locals and visitors alike; nothing special, but good hearty food and all at very reasonable prices.

♥ **Harry Afrika's**, inside Supervalu shopping centre, does grills and the like, and opens on Sun too.

### Annalong

♥♥♥ **Glassdrumman Lodge**, 85 Mill Rd, signposted off the main road at the Newcastle end of the village, **T** 4376 8451, www.glassdrummanlodge.co.uk. This is traditional country food at its best, including local lamb and shellfish. Dinner is £35. See also p117.

## Rostrevor

Rostrevor has a few decent places to eat, better than any in Warrenpoint.

♔ **Celtic Fjord**, 8 Mary St, **T** 4173 8005. Opening times and hours may vary (Wed or Thu to Sat at the moment) but worth a visit for the innovative food and the congenial atmosphere. Dinner menus for £18 and £21 and a good value early dinner for around £9.

♔ **Kilbroney**, Bridge St, **T** 4173 8236. Restaurant in the spacious pub of the same name. Does meals from £9 for fish and chips to £15 for a steak. Traditional music on Wed nights.

## Newry

♔ **The Bank**, 2 Trevor Hill, by the bridge at the tourist office end of town, **T** 3083 5501, www.thebanknewry.com. The new kid on the block. Burgers and salads for lunch around £6 and an evening menu with dishes like tempura monkfish, Cajun pork or grilled aubergine for £8-10. It's a stylish kind of place and brings a bit of glamour to the town as you sit sipping a cocktail at the bar. A nightclub jumps into action here every Fri and Sat night.

♔ **Brass Monkey**, 1 Sandy St, **T** 3026 3176. First choice for a quick meal. Serving seafood, steaks and salads daily till 2200.

♔ **Deli Lites**, 12 Monaghan St. Serves up better-than-average sandwiches.

There are a couple of inexpensive cafés on Hill St, as you walk into the town centre from the tourist office.

# Dundalk and the Cooley Peninsula

## Dundalk

🍴 **Café Metz**, Francis St, Dundalk. Opens for breakfast. €10 lunch, and dinner around €30. Drop in for a coffee and check out the menu.

🍴 **Cube**, easy to find, opposite St Patrick's Cathedral, Dundalk, **T** 042-9329898. A restaurant that very stylishly utilises a Georgian building with original features. Lunch for under €10 if you stay off the seafood, and a choice of evening dishes including a sushi starter. Closed Sun and Mon for dinner.

🍴-🍴 **Number Thirty Two**, 32 Chapel St, Dundalk, **T** 042-933113. Retro-style place serving substantial lunches and a varied menu with dishes like leek sausages, pork and cider, and decent vegetarian choices. The early dinners from 1730 to 1900 are €15-20 and represent excellent value.

🍴 **Courtney's**, Patrick St for light pub food.

🍴 **Derryhale House Hotel**, Carrickmacross Rd, Dundalk (see p120). Both the bar food and the restaurant at this convivial place are reasonably priced, and food from the bar menu can also be enjoyed sitting in the period reception area.

🍴 **The Jockeys**, 47 Anne St, Dundalk. A filling carvery restaurant in this pleasantly situated pub.

## Carlingford

**Ⅲ Ghan House**, Carlingford, **T** 042-9373682,
www.ghanhouse.com. Reservations are essential for the 'set
country-house dinner' (around €50). Fri and Sat only. There's also
a cookery school, which includes accommodation if necessary.

**Ⅱ The Oystercatcher Bistro**, opposite McKevitt's Hotel,
Carlingford, **T** 042-9373922. This place is keen on its seafood.
Oysters are cooked half a dozen different ways, but there's also
Cooley mountain lamb and vegetarian choices.

**Ⅱ-Ⅰ Magee's Bistro**, Tholsel St, Carlingford, **T** 042-9373751. Has
an affordable menu of pizzas and a more formal, restaurant area.

**Ⅰ Georgina's**, a little walk up Castle Hill, Carlingford,
**T** 042-9373346. One place that should not be missed is this modest
little teashop dishing up superb open and regular sandwiches,
perfect cakes such as cream gâteaux or cheesecake, and a
takeaway service. Open all week but closes at 1800.

**Ⅰ Kingfisher Bistro**, in the Heritage Centre, Carlingford,
**T** 042-9373716. Has interesting starters and vegetarians have more
than just a token dish to consider.

**O'Hare's Pub**, Carlingford. Does oysters and Guinness.

! International direct dialling to the Republic of Ireland: 00353.
● Local Dundalk area code: (0)42.

147

# North Antrim Coast

## Portrush

There are some truly dreadful places in the centre of town serving fish-and-chips-type meals; don't be misled by nautical themes and seemingly reasonable prices.

**D'Arcy's**, 92-4 Main St, **T** 7082 2063. Open for lunch, around £7, and dinner around £12-15, with contemporary-style food and lots of fish dishes.

**Ramone Wine Bar**, The Harbour, **T** 7082 4313. Has a menu to suit holiday folk and most dishes are around £10.

**Don Giovanni's**, 9 Causeway St, **T** 70825516. Fine for pizzas and pasta and also does some veal and fish dishes.

## Portrush to Giant's Causeway

**Bushmills Inn**, 25 Main St, Bushmills, **T** 2073 2339. Good food like steak flambéed in a drop of the local hard stuff served at tables privately snuggled around rough, whitewashed stone walls under a low ceiling. Expensive but worth it. See also p122.

**Copper Kettle**, by the roundabout at Bushmills, **T** 2073 2560. 0830-2000 in summer. Serves tea and scones and standard meals around £5-7, and is fine if you are on the move.

**Sweeney's**, Seaport Av, Portballintrae, **T** 2073 2405. A pleasant stone-built pub with a conservatory, and popular sessions of live and loud music on weekend evenings; decent food is served daily 1200-2130.

## Giant's Causeway and around

♈-♈ **Carrick-a-rede**, Ballintoy, **T** 2076 2241. Pub serving food all day in the summer.

♈-♈ **Fullerton Arms**, Ballintoy, **T** 2076 9613. Has a restaurant open 1730-2030, Wed and Sun, in summer. Weekends only in winter.

♈ **Roark's Kitchen**, perched on the rocks at Ballintoy, **T** 2076 3632. Open daily between June and August 1100-1900, and at weekends in May and Sep. Lovely light meals such as buttered mackerel or baked potato with filling for around £3 and lunches listed on a blackboard outside.

## Ballycastle

♈♈ **Glass Island Restaurant**, in the Marine Hotel, 1-3 North St. Has a typical hotel, potato-based menu and is open daily until 2200, while the bar serves snacks.

♈ **Flash in the Pan**, Castle St. An excellent, sit-in or take-out, traditional fish and chip outlet.

♈ **Herald's Restaurant**, 22 Ann St. Next to Wysner's and competing for quick meals and coffee breaks. It comes up with beef, potato and vegetables for £4.

♈ **Wysner's**, 16 Ann St, **T** 2076 2372. This place has won awards for its meat-based dishes and a separate day menu downstairs in the

! If seeking out a local edible seaweed, dulse, go to the Fruit
• Shop in the Diamond, Ballycastle. The shop also stocks yellowman, a chewy toffee eaten hereabouts.

café features bangers and champ (see p133), pasta, and chicken dishes for around £6. Closed Sun.

## Rathlin Island

♟ **Bruce's Kitchen**, at the harbour. Opens daily between 1030 and 2330 for quick fish meals.

Dinner is an option at both **Rathlin Guest House** and **The Manor House** (see p124) but needs booking in advance.

For a picnic on the island stock up with provisions at **Brady's** supermarket in Castle St or the **Co-Op** at the Diamond, Ballycastle.

# Derry

While Derry isn't overrun with exciting restaurants, there are enough places to keep you out of McDonald's during your stay.

♟♟ **Brown's Restaurant**, 2 Bond's Hill, **T** 7134 5180.  *Map 5, p253* Excellent, small menu of innovative dishes in a little converted shop opposite the train station. Popular at lunch time when less than £9 will buy you something you'll remember for days.

♟♟ **Fitzroy's**, 3 Carlisle St,  **T** 7126 6211.  *Map 5, E4, p253*  Open till late daily. A big, popular place, doing inexpensive lunches and a very modern dinner menu – lots of drizzles and pestos. Early dinner menu as well as post-theatre one.

♟♟ **La Sosta**,  45a Carlisle Rd,  **T** 7137 4817.  *Map 5, F4, p253* Tue-Sat, 1830-2200. An authentic, candle-lit, family-run Italian restaurant serving fillet steak, cannelloni, ravioli, and desserts like lime tart with papaya sauce. Good for vegetarians and the atmosphere is friendly.

¶¶ **Mange 2**, 2 Clarendon St, **T** 7136 1222. *Map 5, A3, p253* With starters like mussels and garlic for under £4 and main meat and fish dishes around £13 this a reasonable option. Open for lunch too.

¶ At lunchtime the range of options is much wider with most of the pubs in town doing food of some kind. The pubs along Waterloo St will be busy but they have atmosphere and most do bar grub.

¶ **Café Mezzo**, in Austin's department store, in the Diamond. *Map 5, E3 , p253* Has a large menu, with take-away service, and good for vegetarians. All the food is under £5. Views over the square in the self-service restaurant on the top floor of Austin's help compensate for the predictable meals.

¶ **The Diamond**, in the Diamond. *Map 5, E3, p253* Wetherspoon pub doing cheap food and the cheapest drinks in the city.

¶ **Metro**, Bank Pl, **T** 7126 7401. *Map 5, D4, p253* A little touristy but satisfactory food.

¶ **The Sandwich Company**, 61 Strand Rd, **T** 7126 6771. *Map 5, A3, p253* Popular with lunchtime eaters. There is another branch of this popular shop at the Diamond, **T** 7137 2500.

# Inishowen Peninsula, Donegal

### Fahan and Buncrana

¶¶¶ **St John's Country House and Restaurant**, see p126, **T** 074-9360289. Dinner here begins with drinks in a late 18th-century room with a turf fire burning. The understated menu disguises exquisitely simple dishes, and the fair-priced wine list makes the €40 per head bill money very well spent.

♆ **Railway Tavern**, Fahan, **T** 074-9360137. A bar and restaurant cooking food on an open wood-burning firebox. Opens for dinner Tue-Sun 1800-2200 and for lunch on Sun.

♆ **The Town Clock Restaurant**, 6 Main St, Buncrana, **T** 074-9363279. More of a café, open for breakfast, lunch and dinner.

## Carndonagh

♆♆ **Corncrake Restaurant**, Malin St, on your right leaving the village for Malin, **T** 074-9374534. Serves up a good meal with starters like mussels in cream sauce or crab soufflé and, while Donegal lamb is a speciality, seafood addicts will find something interesting on the menu. This is home-cooking at its best. Vegetarian dishes available but book in advance. Open Tue-Sat, Jun to Sep, but only weekends at other times. Main dishes €18-24.

♆ **The Arch Inn Bar**, in the Diamond, **T** 074-9373029. Serves good bar food and has live music at weekends.

♆ **Boston Burger**, Bridge St. Does what its says over the door – burgers.

♆ **Túl Na Rí** (Simpson's Bar), outside town on the Culdaff road, **T** 074-9374499. An olde-worlde pub serving good food 1230-2200; booking ahead is often necessary to secure an evening table.

**Bridge Street Café**. Soups and sandwiches and take-away menu.

! International direct dialling to the Republic of Ireland: 00353. Local Inishowen Peninsula area code: (0)74.

## Malin and Malin Head

🍴 **Malin Hotel**, Malin Village, **T** 074-9370645. Does bar food and there is an elegant little restaurant in the evening that has a fish, poultry and grill menu. A dish like monkfish with coconut and curry sauce is just under €20.

🍴 **The Cottage**, Malin Head, **T** 074-9370257. Does soup and sandwiches and light meals. Open Jun to Sep 1100-1830 (from 1330 on Sun), and Mar to May Sun only.

🍴 **Seaview Tavern**, Malin Head, **T** 074-9370117. Ireland's most northerly pub. Open daily 0900-2100 for meals.

## Culdaff

**McGrory's**, **T** 074-9379104, www.mcgrorys.ie. Has a restaurant serving seafood as well as meat dishes. It is also worth checking in here to see what is lined up in the way of entertainment (see p166). Open Tue-Sun from 1800. See also Sleeping p127.

## Stroove to Muff

🍴 **Greencastle Fort**, past Greencastle heading towards Muff, **T** 074-9381044. An atmospheric interior in the old fort and does seafood as well as steaks and duck, and the menu is chalked up on blackboards in the spacious bar area.

🍴 **Kealy's Seafood Bar**, Greencastle, **T** 074-9381010. A seafood restaurant on the seafront with a dinner menu for €35, and bar food that includes a delicious chowder. Closed Mon.

Check out...

# WWW...

# Pubs, bars and clubs

Whatever your drinking expectations Belfast has something to offer. The city has excellent pubs especially in some of the little entries which line the main thoroughfares of the centre. Some are all etched glass and mahogany panels, folksy and ancient, while others just look it. Many of them offer live music but there are also quiet locals to drink in. The last few years have seen a burgeoning of ultra cool, minimalist, steel and glass style bars where cash-rich, time-poor Belfast white collar workers eat, drink and chill out. These are predominantly in the city centre and the Cathedral Quarter but there are neat places outside the centre especially in the Lisburn Road and around the university. The Golden Mile abounds with every kind of bar known to man – with huge screen TVs, add-on restaurants and clubs – and at weekends these streets seem to turn into one huge party with little bands roaming from one bar to another and the big friendly bouncers exchanging lively banter with bag ladies and punters alike.

### ★ Best Unreconstructed pubs

- The Crown Liquor Saloon, pages 42 and 158
- White's Tavern, p158
- Kelly's Cellars, p158
- Morning Star, p158
- Madden's, p158

### ...and the coolest bars

- Tatu, p141
- Apartment, p157
- Irene and Nan's, p158
- The Northern Whig, p160
- Kremlin, p205

Most of the city's **clubs** are above pubs in the Golden Mile. They go in and out of fashion and get regular makeovers as fashions change but the Cathedral Quarter is probably where the really cool places are and the Odyssey Pavilion comes recommended. The best place to look for what is on and where is in the free *The Big List* available from cafés, newsagents, rail and bus stations and the tourist office. Also look out for the relatively new *Fate*, also available free in bus and train stations, the airport and cafés.

# City centre

### Pubs and bars

**Apartment**, 2 Donegall Sq West, **T** 9050 9777. *Map 2, F8, p249*
Another style bar with a confusing vocabulary but very hip people. DJs playing an eclectic mix nightly.

**Crown Liquor Saloon**, 46 Great Victoria St , **T** 9024 9476, (see p42). *Map 2, G7, p249* Pride of place in Belfast goes to this old-timer with its authentic decorations and cosy snugs, but you must get here early if you want a seat. The food is good too, sausage and mash and the like.

**Irene and Nan's**, **T** 9023 9123 (see p135). *Map 2, H7, p249* One of the new style bars in the city, it's design based – apparently – on photographs of Prague airport in the 1960s. But a good atmosphere nevertheless. Happy hour Thu and Fri 1700-1900.

**Kelly's Cellars** 30 Bank St. *Map 2, E7, p249* One of the city's oldest pubs, is worth a look in and good for live Irish music. Legend has it that the United Irishmen met here to plan the uprising in 1798.

**Maddens**, Berry St, **T** 9024 4114. *Map 2, E7, p249* An old-fashioned kind of place, full of locals, good for a quiet drink, cheap food  and some live traditional music.

**Morning Star**, 17 Pottinger's Entry, **T** 9032 3976. *Map 2, E9, p249* A listed building and winner of awards for its food. It is quiet at night and a good place for a music, TV and a style-free drink.

**White's Tavern**, Winecellar Entry, **T** 9024 3080. *Map 2, E8, p249* Another ancient pub, which has music upstairs and good pub food on the menu downstairs.

## Clubs

**Limelight**, 17 Ormeau Av, **T** 9032 5942. *Map 2, H8, p249* Beside Katy Daly's pub, this is a serious dance club and has held some major live performances in the city. Tue is 'Shag' – students' night.

**Apartment**
*Mixing with the in crowd at Apartment in Donegall Square...and are those Essex girls in the limo?*

**McHugh's**, 29-31 Queen St, **T** 9050 9990. *Map 2, D10, p249*
Belfast's oldest surviving building, or at least the white part of the building is, the rest being fairly recent additions. The basement bar holds live music sessions of all kinds with traditional music on Thu in the main bar.

**Precious Nite Club**, Odyssey Pavilion, **T** 9046 7089. *Map 2, C12, p249* Holding its own with five dedicated rooms open Thu-Sat.

**Rotterdam Bar**, 54 Pilot St, **T** 9074 6021. *Map 2, B11, p249* The kind of place where beat poets, if they still existed, would hang. Dim, smoky (for now at least!) and filled with live music with a sing song Sun, folk and traditional music Mon, Thu, jazz and blues on Tue, a quiz night Wed, and assorted live bands at weekends.

**Thompsons**, 3 Patterson Pl, off Arthur St, **T** 9032 3762, www.clubthompsons.com. *Map 2, F9, p249* Thu-Sat 2100 till late. A variety of DJ sounds with Sat being the most popular night followed by Fri. Lots of regulars and a wide age range.

# Cathedral Quarter

### Pubs and bars

**The Duke of York**, 11 Commercial Court, **T** 9024 1062. *Map 2, D9, p249* Another of the city's cherished ancient pubs, hidden away down one of the little alleys. Once the hang-out of newspaper types, it has a more varied clientele nowadays with lots of live music sessions including traditional music.

**The Front Page**, Upper Donegall St, **T** 9032 4924, www.thefrontpagebar.com. *Map 2, C8, p249* Live music from Wed to Sun. Generally indie rock.

**The John Hewitt**, 51-53 Donegall St, **T** 9023 3768. *Map 2, D9, p249* A recently built traditional bar which has no TV so people just have to talk to each other. It serves good food and holds regular traditional music, storytelling and jazz sessions.

**The Northern Whig**, 2 Bridge St, **T** 9050 9888 (see p138). *Map 2, E9, p249* There seems to be a tradition in Belfast of importing giant statues from foreign places. Here the city's young and restless sip their cocktails beneath statues of men who once held power over swathes of eastern Europe. Retro café au lait-brown sofas, with DJs starting early on Fri.

## Clubs

**Milk Bar**, Tomb St, **T** 9027 8876. *Map 2, D10, p249* Ferociously fashionable and was voted Northern Ireland's 'Best Small Club' in 2003. Something on every night and Wed is free entrance and two free drinks for women.

# Golden Mile and the University

## Pubs and bars

**Auntie Annie's Porterhouse**, Dublin Rd, **T** 9050 1660. *Map 3, A7, p251* Two floors of bars with a DJ most nights but some interesting live music and occasional poetry readings.

**Botanic Inn**, 23-7 Malone Rd, **T** 9050 9740. *Map 3, F6, p250* Has a student-orientated atmosphere, lots of activities, as if drinking wasn't enough, live music, a big screen TV and some amazing meal deals in the afternoon.

**Eglantine Inn**, 32 Malone Rd, **T** 9038 1994. *Map 3, F6, p250* The other student pub in Malone Rd, with DJs most nights, a pub quiz on Tuesdays and lots of cheap booze offers. Get them young, I always say.

**Empire Basement**, 42 Botanic Av, **T** 9024 9276. *Map 3, B7, p251* Live music, singalong to musical movie scenes, pop quizzes, a salsa night and more.

**Lavery's Gin Palace**, 16 Bradbury Pl, **T** 9087 1106. *Map 3, B7, p251* A vast warren of bars dedicated to alcohol consumption with a clientele that covers the entire spectrum. Just choose the bar that suits you. Upstairs is the Heaven nightclub and there's live music in the Back Bar.

**Morrison's**, 21 Bedford St, **T** 9032 0030. *Map 2, H8, p249* Has live music at weekends and a good atmosphere as well as big screen football matches. Lots of pub food and cool cocktail bar upstairs.

**The Parlour**, Elmwood Av, **T** 9068 6970. *Map 3, D7, p251* A very young place with inexpensive food, fake gas lights and lots of music.

**Weatherspoons**, 35-7 Bedford St. *Map 2, H8, p249* Offers very basic and very inexpensive food and drink.

## Clubs

**The Empire Music Hall**, 42 Botanic Av, **T** 9024 9276. *Map 3, B7, p251* A converted church has something to attract every night but really gets going at the weekends.

**Hell @ Lavery's**, above Lavery's Gin Palace. *Map 3, B7, p251* Popular on Sat nights. Popular on Sat nights with a very young and lively crowd listening to popular local DJs.

**M Club**, 23-5 Bradbury Pl, **T** 9023 3131. *Map 3, C7, p251* Heaves with twentysomething revellers Monday, Thusday and Saturday while Tuesday is student night. Friday is the Sounds of the 70s while Saturday offers current and commercial sounds. Free admission to students early on Thu. Admission prices rise at weekends to £8.

# County Down

### Downpatrick

**The Cabin**, at the bottom of Church St, is a bright airy bar with live music on Sat nights.

**Denvir's** (see p117) has music at weekends, usually country- style folk music or something louder. The other pubs also have live music occasionally.

### Annalong

**The Halfway House**, at the Newcastle end of the village on the main road. Good for a pint and a game of snooker.

### Newry

There are a number of pubs where sessions of traditional Irish music take place throughout the year. Try the following:

**Crossan's Bar**, Hilltown Rd, on Tue nights, **The Forkhill**, Forkhill, on Thu, **O'Hanlon's**, Mullaghbawn, Fri-Sat.

# Dundalk and the Cooley Peninsula

### Dundalk

**Corbetts**, Seatown, Dundalk. Live music on Thursdays.

**Fitzpatrick's**, at Jenkinstown, **T** 042-9376193. A pleasant bar and restaurant.

**Harvey's**, Park St, Dundalk. A big modern pub with sessions every Tuesday night.

**The Jockeys**, 47 Anne St, Dundalk. Traditional Irish music every Friday.

**P McArdle's**, Anne St, Dundalk. With a quieter atmosphere, this place attracts a more purist crowd of performers and audience on the first and third Thu of each month.

**McManus's**, Seatown, Dundalk. Live music on Monday and Friday nights, starting at about 2100.

**Moe's Bar**, close to Courtneys on Park St, Dundalk. Popular beer garden and music most nights.

**Sextons's**, out of town a couple of miles on the Dublin Rd. Enjoy traditional music on Tuesday nights.

**Spirit Store**, by The Harbour, Dundalk, **T** 042-9352697. Very atmospheric music venue; trad, jazz, rock, and world beer on draught.

**Terrace Bar**, Ballymascanlon Hotel (see p119). Music of a non-traditional kind comes alive on Saturday nights and there is also a live band in the ballroom.

## Carlingford

**Lily Finnegan's Pub**, Whitestown, a couple of miles outside Carlingford, on the Dundalk Rd. (Go as far as The Cooley Inn, take a right, pass the church and go through the village. If you hit the beach, you've gone too far.) Good for an atmospheric, quiet drink.

**P J O'Hare's**, aka **the Anchor Bar**, **T** 042-9373106. Still with the old-style grocery/bar division and traditional music on Thursday and jazz on Sunday afternoons.

# North Antrim Coast

### Portrush

On summer nights pubs and hotels are blasting out music, but not of the traditional Irish kind.

**Kelly's**, Bushmills Rd, **T** 7082 6611, www.kellysportrush.com. This is the top club by a mile and its nightclub **Lush!** wins particular acclaim. Visiting DJs include the likes of Fatboy Slim, Pete Tong and Danny Rampling.

### Ballycastle

The tourist board issues a useful directory of what's on, where and when in all the Ballycastle pubs.

**Central Bar**, Ann St, has a regular Wed night session of traditional music that goes al fresco in the summer with the occasional barbecue thrown in for good measure.

**House of McDonnell**. A pub that's been in the same family for over 200 years. Grand for a quiet chat and a drink, and on a Fri night musicians are welcomed.

# Derry

The tourist office dispenses a useful directory of what's on, where and when in the pubs. The other pubs along Waterloo St will have notices up advertising their music nights. For traditional Irish music the bars in Waterloo Street are some of the best. **Peadar O'Donnell's**, **T** 7137 2318, and the **Gweedore**, **T** 7126 3513, close by, are especially recommended. **Bound for Boston**, **T** 7127 1315, usually has live bands Thu-Sat and its **Club Q** has pool tables for £3 an hour. Inside the city walls the **River Inn**, **Downey's** and **Metro** have live music. **Sandino's** is an easy-going, welcome-all pub with music.

# Inishowen Peninsula, Donegal

### Carndonagh

For pub music try **The Persian Bar**, **T** 074-9374823, or the **Sportsman Inn**, **T** 074-9374817, both on the Diamond, or **Bradly's** on Bridge St, **T** 074-9374526.

### Malin and Malin head

**Farren's Bar**, near the weather station and Portmore Pier. Good for a quiet pint.

### Culdaff

**McGrory's**, **T** 074-9379104, www.mcgrorys.ie. A pub serving good food (see p153) but it is also worth checking in here to see what is lined up in the way of entertainment, for some big time performers appear here on a regular basis. Open Tue-Sun from 1800. See also Sleeping p127.

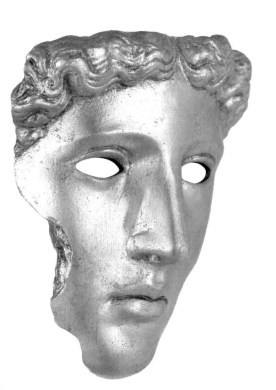

For its size Belfast has a pretty lively arts and entertainments scene. The traditional kind of arts venues such as the Ulster Hall, the Lyric Theatre, the Grand Opera House and the Waterfront Hall are well established and are supplemented by the huge Odyssey Pavilion, by smaller venues at the university, the Old Museum arts centre, St Anne's Cathedral and several of the other churches. Travelling theatre and music performances tend to predominate in the city; for home grown theatre Derry is probably a little richer, although Belfast has its own circus school. Belfasters enjoy the cinema with several big multiplexes and a film festival in Spring. The city is rich in graphic arts – there are several good art galleries which have regular exhibitions, a photographic archive and lots of small private galleries. Perhaps the Troubles were more conducive to art rather than they were to theatre.

For up-to-date listings of events consult the free *The Big List* newspaper, available from the tourist office, rail and bus stations and newsagents.

**Some useful websites**

**www.artslistings.com** All-Ireland arts listings.
**www.linengreen.com** Designer clothing and crafts.
**www.junctionone.co.uk** Designer clothing at reasonable prices.
**www.wheretotonight.com** Live music listings for Ireland.
**www.danceni.com** Dance Northern Ireland.
**www.ulster-orchestra.org.uk** Website of the Ulster Orchestra.
**www.culturenorthernireland.org** Listings on cultural events in Northern Ireland.
**http://cain.ulst.ac.uk/mccormick** The Northern Ireland Mural directory. A tour of Northern Ireland's murals and history. Details of 1500 murals in an impartial survey and 220 images on line.

# Art

### Belfast

Belfast is home to several innovative art galleries displaying regular exhibitions of local artists' work.

**Belfast Exposed**, 23 Donegall Pl, **T** 9023 0965. *Map 2, D9, p249*
A gallery dedicated to photography by local and international photographers whose work focuses on social themes. Besides the exhibitions is a huge collection of archive material recording the social and political history of the city.

**Fenderevsky Gallery**, at the **The Crescent Arts Centre**, 2-4 University Rd, **T** 9024 2338. *Map 3, C7, p251* Has a changing exhibition of local painters.

**Old Museum Arts Centre**, 7 College Sq North, **T** 9023 5053. *Map 2, E7, p249*  Also has varying exhibitions of local artists in what was once the first museum on the island of Ireland. Again, very innovative exhibitions.

**Ormeau Baths Gallery**, 18 Ormeau Av, **T** 9032 1402.  *Map 2, H9, p249*  Four galleries in what was once a public bath house, this place presents more experimental work of both local artists and work in many media from all over Europe.

**W5 exhibition at the Odyssey Pavilion**. *Map 2, C12, p249*  The corridors here are also often filled with some beautiful travelling exhibitions.

Smaller private galleries include: **Safehouse Arts Space**, 25 Donegall St, **T** 9031 4499; **Lawrence St Workshops**, 1a Lawrence St, off Botanic Av, **T** 9023 4993; **Eakin Gallery**, 237 Lisburn Rd, **T** 9066 8522; and the **Mullan Gallery**, 239 Lisburn Rd, **T** 9020 2434; **Raymond Watson**, Conway Mill, west Belfast, **T** 9077 3264, a sculptor whose work is exhibited in the craft shop on the ground floor.

# Cinemas

### Belfast

**The Movie House**, 14 Dublin Rd, and the Yorkgate Centre, 100 York St, **T** 9075 3300. *Map 2, H8, p249*  Multi-screen cineplexes showing the latest Hollywood stuff.

**Queen's Film Theatre**, 7 University Sq Mews, **T** 0800 3282811, www.qub.ac.uk/qft. *Map 3, C7, p251*  The city's art cinema is predictably in the University quarter and good value.

**The craic**
*You won't have to look too hard to find live music in Belfast.*

**Village Cinemas International**, Odyssey Pavilion, **T** 0870 2406020. *Map 2, C12, p249* The city's biggest multiplex.

### Derry

**Orchard Cinema**, Derry, **T** 7126 2845. *Map 5, E5, p253* Derry's film club is housed in St Columb's Theatre. There's also a multiplex with 7 screens **T** 7137 3900.

# Music

### Belfast

**King's Hall**, Balmoral (Lisburn Rd buses), **T** 9066 5225, www.kingshall.co.uk. *Map 1, H2 (off map), p246* Stages the really big rock shows.

**Odyssey Arena**, **T** 9073 9074, www. odysseyarena.com. *Map 2, C12, p249* The city's latest addition to the big concert scene. More commonly home to the Belfast Giants ice hockey team but stepping out for the big names that come to the city.

**Ulster Hall**, Bedford St, **T** 9032 3900. *Map 2, G8, p249* Hosts classical performances by the Ulster Orchestra as well as some rock concerts.

**Waterfront Hall**, Lanyon Pl, **T** 9033 4455. *Map 2, F11, p249* Hosts a whole range of events from classical music to school parents' evenings, stand-up gigs by ageing comics, ballet, jazz, and big name pop stars.

Other places which occasionally play host to classical music are: **St Anne's cathedral** (see p47), the **Linenhall Library** (see p35), **Clonard Monastery** (see p58) and the **Mandela Hall**, Queen's University Students' Union, **T** 9023 6057.

There are very few pubs in the city that don't have music of some kind or a late-night club attached somewhere (see Pubs, bars and clubs chapter, p157). See this section for pubs that have live music in other parts of the country covered in the book too.

# Theatre

### Belfast

**Grand Opera House**, Great Victoria St, **T** 9024 1919. *Map 2, G7, p249* Worth a visit just for the decorations, but it regularly has big-name shows transferred from Dublin or London's West End.

At a time when no one wanted to know about Ireland and its culture, a relatively unknown writer, Brian Friel, and a very unknown actor, Stephen Rea, formed a theatre group called the Field Day Theatre company in Derry. They attracted the co-operation of other writers and people in the arts – Tom Paulin, Seamus Deane (a poet who later became the director of Field Day), David Hammond the film maker, and the poet Seamus Heaney. Situated on the border of the two states, with the benefit of two cultural traditions, Catholic and Protestant, Field Day offered writers and audiences a "Fifth Province", a place where it was safe to look at what Ireland was without breaking cultural taboos. One of its first successes was Friel's *Translations*, which was performed in the Guildhall in Derry and then went on tour around Ireland with Stephen Rea and Liam Neeson in its cast, playing in school halls to audiences of farmers who recognized its cultural significance. Throughout the 1980s Field Day grew in reputation, putting on productions by Friel, Tom Kilroy, Stewart Parker and Terry Eagleton, and producing pamphlets on all aspects of Irish culture, culminating in 1991 in the *Field Day Anthology of Irish Writing*, which sadly left out most women writers (redressed in 2002 with two new volumes).

**Lyric Theatre**, off Ridgeway St, which is off Stranmillis Rd south of the city, **T** 90381081. *Map 3, G8, p251* The city's serious theatre. It regularly has important modern productions. There is a student standby scheme where remaining tickets will be sold off at reduced prices to students after 1930 on the night of the production.

**Old Museum Arts Centre**, College Sq North, **T** 9023 3332. *Map 2, E7, p249*  Arts centre with a small theatre where the avant garde can be found.

---

## Derry

**Guildhall**, see p99. *Map 5, C4, p253*  Since the Bloody Sunday Inquiry has finished, the Guildhall hosts orchestral concerts and the like.

**Millennium Forum**, Newmarket St, **T** 7216 0516, www.milleniumforum.co.uk. *Map 5, D4, p253*  A regular schedule of local productions and touring theatre groups.

**Nerve centre**, 7-8 Magazine St, **T** 7126 6946, www.nerve-centre.org.uk. *Map 5, D3, p253*  A performance venue, café and cinema as well as lots of very arty stuff.

**Playhouse**, 5-7 Artillery St, **T** 7126 8027, www.derryplayhouse.co.uk. *Map 5, E4, p253*  Another multimedia venue, where at various times you can catch art exhibitions, theatre, dance and concerts.

**Verbal Arts Centre**, near Bishop's Gate, **T** 7126 6946, www.verbartscentre.co.uk. *Map 5, F2, p253*  Worth a visit just to see the beautifully renovated former Blue Coat School (1894) and the glass sculpture by Killian Schuman which contains manuscripts donated by Ireland's many writers. The place is an archive of stories and poetry collected from storytellers and poets around Ireland and there is a lively programme of events well worth checking out. Mon-Thu 0900-1700, Fri 0900-1600.

Belfast has some increasingly important arts and cultural festivals and the glory of them is that unlike Dublin, where it's standing room only everywhere you go and the fiddly diddly music will turn you cross-eyed eventually, in Belfast festivals are still very much a local event. Visiting during a festival time won't mean booking months in advance and putting up with crowds of tourists. St Patrick's Day passes by pretty much unnoticed except in Downpatrick and Derry, while April brings the Belfast Film Festival, not as big as Dublin but perhaps a more radical outlook. The Orange Parades still figure large in July although there is a more laid back atmosphere than there ever was in the past when things often got frighteningly tense. The West Belfast festival gets bigger every year and is genuinely cross-cultural. Derry is a good place to head in April for its jazz festival, in October and November for its film festival and some great Halloween events. Other places to look out for are Carrickfergus Lughnasa celebrations, The Ulster American Folk Park for the Bluegrass festival and the Oul Lammas Fair in Ballycastle.

## February

**Derry INSTINCT - Young People's Festival**, T 7126 0562, www.nerve-centre.org.uk. Early Feb. A multi-media, video, drama, clay-modelling and a variety of workshops for the under 18s.

## March

**St Patrick's Day** (17th March). This is the big event of the year in Downpatrick, which is extended into a week of cross-cultural activities that attract large crowds. Not so stunning in the rest of the north.

**City of Derry Drama Festival**, Millennium Forum, Newmarket St, T 71264455, www.millenniumforum.co.uk. A week in early March. Theatre festival with performances, street theatre and workshops.

**J20 Big Tickle Comedy Festival**, The Playhouse Theatre, Artillery St, Derry, T 71268027, www.derryplayhouse.co.uk. Two weeks in early March. Lots of stand up comedy, theatre, big names from the UK.

## April

**Belfast Film Festival**, Exchange Place, 23 Donegall St, T 9032 5913, www.belfastfilmfestival.org. In early April this festival includes film classics, cult movies and new Irish and international films shown at venues around the city. Includes a drive-in movie, workshops in film making, music sessions, seminars and discussions.

**City of Derry Jazz and Big Band Festival T** 7137 6545, www.cityofderryjazzfestival.com. Five days in late April-early May.

Established as Northern Ireland's leading event of its kind. 2005 includes Van Morrison.

**Festival of Fools**, Belfast Community Circus School, 23/25 Gordon St, Belfast, **T** 9023 6007, www.foolsfestival.com. This runs from noon till early evening in venues throughout the city centre and is Ireland's only festival of street theatre. Includes juggling, clowns, acrobats, and walking performers wandering the streets.

## May

**Cathedral Quarter Arts Festival**, 43 Donegall St, Belfast, **T** 9023 2403, www.cqaf.com. Now in its sixth year, the Cathedral Quarter festival involves 10 days (in early May) of music, theatre, comedy, circus, art exhibitions, talks, discussions, exhibitions by new and established artists and street events. It comes highly recommended.

**Belfast Marathon**, PO Box 39, Belfast, BT32 8BL, **T** 9027 0345, www.belfastcitymarathon.com. In early May. The Belfast Marathon itself attracts over 1,200 competitors, many of them international competitors, while the Marathon Walk, Marathon Team Relay and Fun Run increase the total number of runners to over 10,000.

**Belfast Summer in the City**, **T** 9027 0222, late May-Sep. Includes all kinds of events from local stuff to major concerts, including the Lord Mayor's Show.

**Blues on the Bay Festival**, Warrenpoint. Contact: Ian Sands, Bay Blues Project, c/o 13 Cherry Hill, Rostrevor, Co Down, BT34 3BD. The Blues festival includes over 50 shows in late May, many of them free.

**Waterfront guitarist**
*Festival time in the North brings folk from all over the world (and beyond?) to participate. Here a strange creature rehearses outside the Waterfront Hall.*

## July

**Orange Marches**. Basically the city goes pretty quiet for the first two weeks in July around the height of the marching season. This culminates on the 12th when several formerly contentious parades which once marched through Catholic communities still take place in a foreshortened and agreed way.

**Inishowen Agricultural Show**, in the middle of July each year in Carndonagh, has competitions with judging of sheep, cattle and horses in the morning and family activities during the afternoon. There's also a street festival that takes place later in the month. (See also the Sights section p100 for more local festivals in the area.)

**Belfast Pride**, www.2005@belfastpride.com, is a week-long gay pride festival in late July-early August and includes a parade, pub quizzes, parties and the like.

**Lughnasa**, 24th July, is celebrated at Carrickfergus castle with Punch and Judy, harvest festival, archery, sword fighting displays, drumming and theatre groups.

## August

**Ardoyne Fleadh**, **T** 9075 1056. Three days of open-air concerts and community events in north Belfast, in early August.

**Féile an Phobail**, **T** 9031 3440, www.feilebelfast.com. Currently in its 18th year this festival is recognized as one of the biggest community organized festivals in Europe. Originally a tiny carnival and parade for children of the Falls Road, the festival now draws international poets, stand up comics, theatre groups and more in both the Falls Road marquee and to venues around west Belfast. It is celebrated as an inclusive, non-sectarian event and takes place during the first two weeks in August and includes street parties, concerts, Irish-language events and a carnival parade. Previous attendees include Martin Sheen, Mar Macaleese, Gerry Adams and Michael McGimpsey, minister for arts culture and leisure.

**Northern Ireland Kite Festival**, Portstewart Strand. Contact Robert Patton, Beach Manager, Portstewart Strand, **T** 7083 6369. A weekend in late August. Professional kite flyers, giant kites, a Chinese dragon kite competition, aerial sculptures, parachuting teddy bears, synchronized flying, fighting kites, power kiting. Also bouncy castles, children's entertainers, face painting etc.

**Oul' Lammas Fair**, on the last Mon and Tue of August in Ballycastle, Co Antrim, has a good claim to be Ireland's oldest traditional fair and is a very lively event with a market, music, dancing, and more.

## September

**Fiddlestone Arts and Cultural Festival**, Belleek, contact Eileen O'Toole, Festival Co-ordinator, **T** 6865 9701, eiotoole@yahoo.com. 10 days in early September. Music and crafts in the pretty little village of Belleek right on the border with the Republic. Events in the Fiddlestone pub and the Carlton Hotel with a street parade, cookery demonstrations, guided bus and walking tours, art exhibitions, dance workshops, storytelling, a re-enactment of an American wake.

## October

**Two Cathedrals Festival**, Derry. Contact Dermot Carlin, **T** 7126 8335. The largest and noisiest of festivals in Derry. Two weeks of classical music in the two cathedrals and other venues plus more down to earth stuff too. It takes place in mid-October and is followed by a week or so of fireworks and fun at Halloween. Look out for the Halloween tours at this time of year, they're great fun.

**South Armagh Hill-walking festival**, South Armagh Festival Events Office, Main St, Camloch, **T** 30837 0576. The South Armagh Hill Walking Festival takes place over the first weekend in October. The Walking Weekend has gained a lot of interest both locally and nationally.

---

## November

**Belfast Festival at Queen's**, **T** 9066 7687 for information, **T** 9027 2626 for bookings, www.belfastfestival.com. Two weeks in late October-early November. Established 42 years ago this is Ireland's largest arts festival with 400-plus shows during three weeks around November, based around Queen's University, the Waterfront Hall, Grand Opera House, Ormeau Baths Gallery and the Lyric Theatre as well as smaller arts centres, community venues, pubs and hotels. Belfast's answer to the Edinburgh Festival.

**The Foyle Film Festival** Derry, 7-8 Magazine St, **T** 7126 7432, www.foylefilmfestival.com. 10 days in early November. Talks, competitions, screenings, international and Irish short films, animations, digital live actions.

Shopping

Belfast is similar to every other United Kingdom shopping centre, with its pedestrianized streets, lookalike malls and big chain stores, but at least it is in the city centre and not out in some disused quarry or beside a motorway. The main shopping area is around Donegall Place, Royal Avenue and the Fountain area. Parking is simple enough in the centre, with lots of well marked car parks, and many of the big shops open on Sunday afternoons. All shops are closed on Easter Day and on Sunday and Monday when 12 July falls on a Sunday. The Castlecourt Shopping Centre is right in the middle of the pedestrianized area and bursts with British names, including Debenhams. North of the centre is the Yorkgate Centre with more shops, and smaller, less prosperous malls lurk around town. Soon to dominate the city centre (in 2007) will be the new Victoria Centre which promises to bring in some really big British names.

## Opening hours

Most shops in Belfast open seven days a week, throughout the year, opening at around 0900 until 1800 or later. On Sunday, shops in the city centre at least open at 1300 while parking in the city centre is less expensive than during the week. Again in the city Center shops stay open until around 2100 on Thu.

## Antiques

Donegall Pass is the best place for looking for curios and more expensive items. Particular local souvenirs of the area are the many pottery representations of King Billy on his white horse.

**Alexander the Grate**, 110 Donegall Pass, **T** 9023 2041. *Map 3, B8, p251* Mostly antique fireplaces but also has an antiques market on Saturday.

**Archives**, 88 Donegall Pass, **T** 9023 2383. *Mon-Fri 1030-1730. Map 3, B7, p251* Big place with more affordable items from old pub fittings to King Billy statues.

**Oakland Antiques**, 135-137 Donegall Pass, **T** 9023 0176. *Mon-Sat 1000-1730. Map 3, B8, p251* Biggest of the Donegall Pass bunch with everything from large bits of furniture to silver nick nacks.

**Petite Antiques**, 123 York St, **T** 9064 4632, enquiries@petite antiques.com. *Map 2, B9, p249* Clocks, music Boxes, figurines, dolls, glassware, jewellery, oil lamps circa 18th and 19th century.

## Art galleries

**Green Cross Art and Bookshop**, 51-55 Falls Rd, **T** 9024 3371. *Mon-Sat 0930-1730. Map 2, F2, p248* Local art and some interesting books.

**Workshops Collective**, 1a Lawrence St, **T** 9020 0707. *Mon-Fri 1030-1730, Sat 1130-1600.* *Map 3, B7, p251* Series of workshops where you can visit the artists at work and buy some of their stuff. Paintings, furniture, crafts and more.

## Arts and crafts

**Belfast Crystal Factory**, Kennedy Way, **T** 9062 2051, www.belfastcrystal.com. *Mon-Fri 0930-1700.* *Map 1, G1 (off map, p246* Established only in 1978 this factory outlet shop sells lead crystal: from glasses to paperweights and all in between. Special commissions taken.

**Catherine Shaw**, 25-27 Queen's Arcade, **T** 9032 6053. *Mon-Sat 0930-11715, Thu 0930-1845.* *Map 2, F8, p249* Jewellery, glasses, vases, watches, clocks etc, all in the classical style of Charles Rennie MacKintosh, the famous Glasgow artist.

**Conway Mill**, ground floor Conway Mill, see p57. *Open from about 1000-1500.* *Map 2, E2, p248* Has the work of local craftspeople, most of them with workshops in the mill buildings.

**Craftworks**, Bedford House, Bedford St. *Map 2, H8, p249* Has beautiful handmade clothes and craft objects from all over Ireland.

**Natural Interior**, 51 Dublin Rd, **T** 9024 2656. *Map 2, A7, p249* Irish-linen throws, trimmed in velvet, by the designer Larissa Watson-Regan. It also stocks her vividly coloured wall panels and cushions.

**Ogham Gallery**, 497 Antrim Rd, **T** 9077 2580. *Map 1, D4, p246* Sells locally made craft items such as bodhrans, carved bog oak and hand crafted slate items.

**Donegall Place**
*Temples to old and new money. 21st-century Donegall Place with the 19th-century City Hall in the background.*

**Open Window Productions**, 1-3 Exchange Pl, **T** 9032 9669. *Map 2, B9, p249* Buy 12-inch-high puppets of Northern Ireland politicians for £175. You can have a puppet made to order of a favourite celebrity, or even of yourself.

**Global Creations**, Fountain Centre. *Map 2, F7, p249* Sells craft objects from a round the world selling at fair trade prices.

**Smyth's Irish Linens**, 65 Royal Av, **T** 9024 2232. *Map 2, D8, p249* Linen handkerchiefs, tablecloths, napkins, and other traditional goods. Opposite Castle Court Shopping Centre.

**The Steensons**, next door to Craftworks in Bedford House, Bedford St. *Map 2, H8, p249* Makers of exquisite, reasonably priced silver jewellery. Their own creations plus the work of others.

**The Wicker Man**, Donegall Arcade, **T** 9024 3550. *Map 2, E8, p249* Belfast's biggest craft shop with the work of over 150 craftspeople from all over the island in stock. This is a tiny shop which bursts with good stuff to buy so ask for assistance if there's something you specifically want.

## Books

The regular bookshops can be found in the city centre: **Waterstones**, 8 Royal Av, *Map 2, E8, p249*, **Dillons**, 42 Fountain St, *Map 2, F8, p249*, **Eason's**, 16 Ann St, *Map 2, E9, p249*. Other more specialist dealers are listed below.

**An Leathrá Póilí**, 513 Falls Rd. *Map 1, G1 (off map), p246* Has books on Irish issues from a Republican perspective. Also has a café.

**Ex Libris**, Unit 28, Victoria Centre. *Map 2, G7, p249* Has a large stock of second-hand material and sells graphic novels.

**Familia Bookshop**, 64 Wellington Pl. *Map 2, F7, p249* Good selection of titles and has books on Irish issues.

**Roma Ryan's**, 73 Dublin Rd. *Map 3, B7, p251* Has prints and rare, second hand and antique books.

Two private dealers are:
**Emerald Isle Books**, 539 Antrim Rd, **T** 9037 0798, and **P&B Rowan**, Carleton House, 92 Malone Rd, **T** 9066 6448. Appointments are necessary at both.

## Clothes and accessories

**BT9/Paul Costelloe**, 45 Bradbury Pl, T 9023 9496. *Mon-Sat 0930-1730, Thu 0900-2100. Map 3, B7, p251* Famous Irish designer, Paul Costelloe. Look out for jackets, and Irish linen. Other designers are represented here too: Rachel Mackey, Gerard Darel and Nicole Fahri. Very expensive but look out for the sales when it all gets reduced by as much as 75%.

**Clark and Dawe**, 485 Lisburn Rd, **T** 9066 8228. *Map 3, F3, p250* Make and sell men's and women's suits and shirts.

**Fresh Garbage**, 24 Rosemary St, **T** 9024 2350. *Map 2, E8, p249* Mon-Sat 1030-1730. Some women's clothes with attitude but mostly lovely hand crafted silver jewellery in Celtic designs. Lots of things to insert into your piercings. Hippies and bikers will love it.

**Liberty Blue**, Lombard St, **T** 9059 7555. *Map 2, E8, p249* Retro fashion. Levi 501s, leather jackets, 70s shirts, cords, combats at reasonable prices. Well presented memorabilia clothing.

**Long Tall Sally**, 73 Royal Av, **T** 9032 7710. *Mon-Sat 0930-1730, Thu till 2130. Map 2, D8, p249* Everything for the taller, longer woman at reasonable prices, from maternity wear to cool boots, bikinis to hiking gear.

**Peel**, 107 Bloomfield Av, **T** 9045 2665. *Mon-Sat 0930-1730*. Very cool designer items for the thin and lovely. Lovely shoes.

**Rojo**, 613 Lisburn Rd, **T** 9066 6998. *Mon-Sat 0930-1730*. *Map 3, G2, p250*  Designer footwear from some of the best: Prada, Armando Pollini, Luc Benjen, Gucci, Chanel, DKNY, Stuart Weitzman and Kenzo. January sees many of the items become almost affordable in the annual sale.

**The Rusty Zip**, 28 Botanic Av, **T** 9024 9700. *Mon-Sat 1000-1800*. *Map 3, B7, p251*  Retro clothes from the 60s and 70s – wigs too – all in an interior bedecked with zebra stripes and psychedelia.

**Ryalto**, 591 Lisburn Rd, **T** 9066 7765. *Mon-Sat 1000-1700*. *Map 3, G2, p250*  Expensive European labels: Jocabi, Prima, Natalie Chaize, Ana Sousa, Mamut and more. Shop here and fear not the embarrassment of turning up at the do wearing the same thing as someone else.

**Smyth and Gibson**, Bedford House, Bedford St, **T** 9023 0388. *Map 2, H8, p249*  Make and sell linen and cotton shirts and accessories.

## Food

**The Arcadia**, 378 Lisburn Rd, **T** 9038 1779. *Map 1, H2 (off map), p246*  Old, established delicatessen where you could just stand and admire the products lining the walls. Sandwiches, fresh olives, strange sausages and more.

**Gourmet Ireland Ltd**, 7 Leslie House, Shaftesbury Av, **T** 0870 178 9800. *Mon-Fri 0900-1700*. *Map 3, B7, p251*  Owned by the Rankins, the proprietors of many of the city's good places to eat. The shop sells a range of gift hampers full of lovely things to scoff.

**Nutmeg**, 9a Lombard St, **T** 9024 9984. *Mon-Sat 0930-1730. Map 2, E8, p249* Tiny health food shop selling all manner of for dried fruit, vitamins and other veggie stuff. Also has a good alternative message board.

## Markets

**St George's Market**, May St. *Map 2, G10, p249* This market has existed for many years and has undergone major renovations recently. It is still a fruit and vegetable market, but also has stalls selling bric-à-brac, second-hand and new clothes, and on Friday has more than 200 stallholders. It is also home to a twice monthly Saturday farmers' market.

## Miscellaneous

**The Gadget Shop**, Castle Court Shopping Centre, **T** 0800 7838343. *Map 2, D/E8, p249* Things for the boys. All kinds of gadgets to give as gifts.

**War on Want**, 24 Botanic Av, **T** 9024 7773. *Mon-Sat 1030-1630. Map 3, B7, p251* Charity shop selling all the usual donated stuff as well as good fair trade coffee, ecologically sound washing powder, loads of cheap paperbacks, etc.

## Shopping centres

**Castlecourt Shopping Centre**, Royal Av, **T** 9023 4591. *Mon-Sat 0900-800, Thu 0900-2100, Sun 1300-1800. Map 2, D/E8, pXXX* Debenhams is here, as is the wonderful T K Maxx, full of everything from geekwear to costly designer stuff all at excellent prices.

**Queen's Arcade**, T 9024 6609. *Mon-Fri 0730-2300, Sat 0800-2300. Map 2, F8, p249*  This is the classiest arcade in the city centre, with lots of jewellery shops. In particular **Lunn's**, **Lauren May Jewellery** and **Catherine Shaw** are good places to stock up on your diamonds. **The Perfume Box** is an interesting place and also here is the enormous and popular **Queen's Café Bar**.

**Yorkgate Shopping Centre**, York Rd, T 9074 0990. *Mon-Sat 0900-1800, Sun 1000-1800. Map 2, A10, p249*

### Sporting goods

**Millets**, Cornmarket. *Map 2, E9, p249*  Usual collection of sportswear and camping equipment.

**Surf Mountain**, 12 Brunswick St. *Map 2, G7, p249*  Specializes in surfing, skateboarding and snowboarding gear but also has an excellent collection of camping equipment.

**Tiso**, 12-14 Cornmarket St, T 9023 1230. *Mon, Tue, Fri Sat 0930-1730, Wed 1000-1730 Thu 0900-2000. Map 2, E9, p249*  Camping gear, walking boots, rainwear etc.

Spectator sports are the name of the game for most Belfast people. Increasingly popular is politically neutral ice hockey, with the Belfast Giants playing teams from mainland Britain on Saturday nights through the Autumn. In the city itself football is the spectator sport of choice with local football teams relatively ignored in favour of televised games from the mainland. Belfast football supporters support two Glasgow football teams, Celtic (Cathlolic) and Rangers (Protestant) with all the sectarian brouhaha that goes with it. Manchester United and Liverpool also fit into the sectarian mix. Local teams are also strictly sectarian in nature. Gaelic games, hurling and Gaelic football can be seen in the city at Roger Casement Park in Andersonstown while rugby is also popular. And if you feel restless after all the spectating, there are activities enough to engage in: swimming, surfing, fishing, walking, off-road driving, horse riding, scuba and skydiving.

## Adventure sports

**Blue Lough Mountain and Water Sports Centre**, The Corncrake Building, Lower Sq, Castlewellan, Co Down, **T** 4377 0715. Open all year. Water- and land-based adventure sports from sea kayaking to orienteering and bouldering. Tuition and hire. Also organize trips around Ireland.

**Carlingford Adventure Centre**, **T** 042-9373100, www.carlingfordadventure.com. Land-and water-based activities.

**Helicopter Training and Hire Ltd**, Newtownards Airfield, 28 Comber Rd, Newtownards, Co Down, BT23 4QP, **T** 9182 0028, www.helicoptercentre.co.uk. Does what it says on the label: helicopter flying lessons or pleasure trip hire.

**Land Rover Experience NI**, Clandeboye Courtyard, Bangor, **T** 0870 264 4457, www.landrover.co.uk. Off-road driving, quad bikes and Landrovers.

**Outdoor Ireland North**, 14 Shimnavale, Newcastle, Co Down, BT33 0EF, **T** 43725191, www.outdoorirelandnorth.co.uk. Guided walking, trekking and cycling trips.

**Surfin Dirt All Terrain Boarding**, track address Tullyree Rd, Bryansford, mailing address: 21 Fofanny Rd, Kilcoo, Co Down, **T** 07739 210119, www.surfindirt.co.uk. £10 per hour including training. Lower prices for proficient riders. Mountain boarding is a mix of surfing and snowboarding. This is an official Maxtrack site, and they are the pioneers of mountain boarding in the UK and Europe. A mountain boarding festival is scheduled for the weekend of 23rd and 24th July 2005.

**Táin Adventure Centre**, Carlingford, **T** 042-9375385, www.tainvillage.com.

**Todds Leap Activity Center**, Todds Leap Rd, Ballygawley, Co Tyrone, **T** 8556 7170. Huge range of activities involving toys for the boys: Land Rovers, quad bikes, go karts, archery equipment, indoor rifle range, assault course, excavator (don't ask!), clay pigeon shooting. Packages range around £160 per person inclusive of dinner, bed and breakfast.

**The Wild Geese Skydiving Centre**, Wild Geese Skydiving Centre, Movenis Airfield, 116 Carrowreagh Rd, Garvagh, Coleraine, Co Derry, BT51 5LQDZ, **T** 2955 8609, www.wildgeese.demon.co.uk. Skydiving lessons, tandem skydives. Prices £170-270 for a full day's training.

## Cycling

**Lifecycles**, Unit 35 Smithfield market, Belfast, **T** 9043 9959. *Map 2, D7, p249* Hire bikes and organise city and country tours.

**Millennium National Cycling Network**, **T** 9025 3000 has information about cycling routes.

**Pedal Power Ireland**, **T** 9071 5000, www.pedalpowercycleireland.co.uk. Cycling tours and hire.

## Diving

**Aquaholics**, 14 Portmore Road, Portstewart, BT55 7BE, **T** 70832584, www.aquaholics.org. Full range of courses from Open Water to Divemaster. All equipment provided. 9m Redbay Cabin covers the whole north coast of Ireland from Tory Island to Malin Head to Rathlin Island and the Western Scottish Isles. RIB is available for trips along Giants Causeway.

**D V Diving**, 138 Mountstewart Road, Newtownards, County Down, BT22 2ES, **T** 91 464671, info@dvdiving.co.uk. DV Diving offer scuba, technical and commercial diving and powerboat training courses for the complete beginner through to instructor in the waters around County Down. Explore wrecks, or discover the marine life of Strangford Lough.

## Fishing

**Enagh Trout Lake**, 12, Judges Rd, Derry, **T** 7186 0916.

**The Loughs Agency**, 22 Victoria Rd, Derry, **T** 7134 2100. Information and licences.

## Football

**Irish Football League**, Belfast, **T** 9024 2888, www.irishfa.com. Ring for details of matches.

There are regular matches in Belfast at **Seaview**, off Shore Rd, home ground of the Crusaders; the **Oval**, Redcliffe Pde, in the Newtownards Rd, home ground of Glentoran; and **Solitude**, Cliftonville, the home ground of Cliftonville. International matches are held at **Windsor Park** near the Lisburn Rd, the home of Linfield Park Football Club, **T** 9024 4198.

## Gaelic Football

Matches at weekends at **Roger Casement Park**, Andersonstown Rd, Belfast, **T** 01232 613661, 01232-213490. 1000-1600 for information. Northern Ireland teams take part in the All-Ireland competition. For details of fixtures in all Gaelic Games call the **Gaelic Athletic Association**, **T** 9038 3815.

## Greyhound racing

**Brandywell Greyhound Racing Co**, Brandywell Football ground, Derry, **T** 7126 5461.

## Horse riding

**Drumgooland House**, **T** 4481 1956, www.horsetrek-Ireland.co.uk.

**Maddybenny Riding Centre**, 18 Maddybenny Park, Portrush, **T** 7082 3394.

**West Gate Riding Stables**, Colin Glen Forest park, **T** 01232 615096/202851. Pony trekking in the Colin Glen Forest park. Lessons for all ages and proficiency.

## Hurling

Weekends, **Roger Casement Park**, Belfast. **T** 01232 613661, **T** 01232 213490 *1000-1600 for information*. Northern Ireland won the junior All Ireland hurling championship in 2002 so expect quality games. Ulster hurling final is held here in May.

## Ice hockey

**Belfast Giants**, play at the Odyssey Arena, **T** 9059 1111, advance booking **T** 9073 9074, www.belfastgiants.co.uk.  *Map 2, C12, p249*

## Ice skating

**Ice Bowl**, 111 Old Dundonald Rd, Belfast, **T** 90482611. *Ice rink Mon-Thu 1100-1700, 1930-2200, Fri 1100-1700, 1730-2200, Sat, Sun 1000-1200, 1300-1700, 1730-2200. Ulsterbus 511 from*

Laganside Bus Centre. Adult £4, children £3, skate hire £1.
Olympic-sized rink.

---

### Leisure centres and swimming pools

**Andersonstown Leisure Centre**, Andersonstown Rd, Belfast,
BT119BG, **T** 9062 5211. *Map 1, G1 (off map), p246* Mon-Fri
0830-2200, sat Sun 1000-1600. Prices vary according to activity. Off
peak rates 0900-1700. 3 pools, fitness centre, various courts.

**Brooke Park Leisure Centre**, Rosemont Av, Derry, **T** 7126 2637.
Squash, fitness training, sauna, tennis, bowls.

**Carlingford Adventure Centre**, **T** 042-9373100,
www.carlingfordadventure.com. Land-and water-based activities.

**Belfast Giants**
*It's not just Gaelic sports that are popular here. Ice hockey has an
impressive following too.*

**Shankill Leisure Centre**, 100 Shankill Rd, Belfast, **T** 9024 1434. *Map 1, E3, p246*  Mon-Fri 0830-2200, Sat Sun 1000-1600. Prices vary according to activity. Off peak between 0900-1700. Includes 'Water Wonderland' a leisure pool.

**Lisnagelvin Leisure Centre**, in the Waterside, Derry, **T** 7134 7695. Pool, wave-making machine.

**Olympia Leisure Centre**, Boucher Rd, Belfast, **T** 9023 3369. Mon-Fri 1000-2200, Sat, Sun 1000-1600. Prices vary according to activity. Off peak 0900-1700.

**Táin Adventure Centre**, Carlingford, **T** 042-9375385, www.tainvillage.com.

**Templemore Sports Complex**, Buncrana Rd, Derry, **T** 7126 5521. Pools, sauna, squash, major sporting events in the main sports hall.

### Motor racing

**Ulster Grand Prix**, takes place at Dunrod, to the west of Belfast, each August, and racing also takes place at Kirkistown, **T** 9064 9141 and Bishopscourt, **T** 4484 2202.

### Rugby

**Collegians**, Harlequins, Deramore Park, Malone Rd or Ormeau Gdns, Ormeau Rd, Belfast, **T** 9020 2027. Home grounds to the AIB First Division rugby team Harlequins.

**Malone Rugby Club**, Malone Park, Gibson Park Av, Belfast, BT6 9GN, **T** 90451312, www.malone-rfc.com. AIB third division games.

**Ravenhill Grounds**, 85 Ravenhill Park, Belfast, **T** 9049 3222. *Map 1, H6, p246* The ground where the Ulster Rugby team play international matches. **Irish Rugby Football Union**, **T** 9064 9141, www.ulsterrugby.com, gives details of fixtures, or check the local papers for listings.

## Sailing

**Carlingford Yacht Charter and Seaschool**, **T** 042-9373878, and **Dundalk and Carlingford Sailing Club**, **T** 042-9373238. Courses and yacht chartering.

## Surfing

**Troggs**, 88 Main St, Portrush, **T** 7082 5476. Has all the gear and advice.

## Swimming

See Leisure centres above.

## Tennis

**Belfast Tennis Arena**, Ormeau Embankment, **T** 9045 8024. *Map 3, A12, p251* Mon-Sat 0900-2200, Sun 1000-1800. Court Hire £16.50. Off peak rates Mon-Fri 0900-1700. Indoor tennis courts as well as climbing wall.

## Ten-pin bowling

**Ice Bowl**, 11 Old Dundonald Rd, Belfast, **T** 9048 2611. Daily 1000-2200. 30 lanes, 5 miles out of city. Extreme Bowling with flashing lights and music Fri from 1600, Sat, Sun from 1400.

**Odyssey Bowl**, Odyssey Pavilion, Belfast, **T** 9046 7030. *Map 2, C12, p249* Mon-Wed, Fri 1600-0100, Thu 1000-0200, Sat Sun 1100-0100. £18 per lane per hour, £3.50 per person.

**Superbowl**, 4 Clarence St West, off Bedford St, Belfast, **T** 9033 1466. *Map 2, H8, p249*

## Walking

**Ulster Way** The total length is around 560 miles (900 km), so choices have to be made. Sections following the north Antrim coast, the Glens of Antrim, and the Mourne Mountains (called the Mourne Trail) are the best, plus the 69-mile (111 km) Donegal section. Advance planning is necessary: The Northern Ireland Tourist Board has information on sections and Paddy Dillon's book (see p235) should be consulted. See also the Mourne Mountains section, p74.

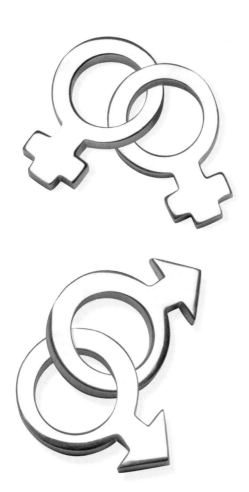

In Northern Ireland, as in the rest of Britain, homosexuals enjoy an equal status with heterosexuals under the law. The age of consent is 16 for men and women and, in 2003, a law prohibiting the promotion of homosexuality in schools was repealed. What the law says and what happens in practice often differ, however, and it would be fair to say that the north of Ireland is less tolerant of gay lifestyles than, say, Dublin or London. One or two protestant sects have complained that their human rights are being eroded by public displays of gayness and there has been a rise in the number of attacks on gay men in Belfast, although it is unlikely that being gay here is any more dangerous than in any other major city. There are several gay and lesbian social and support groups in Belfast, Newry, Derry and Donegal. Lots of gay people travel to Dublin for the weekend but the gay scene in Belfast changed a few years ago, with the opening of Kremlin and several related bars and gay-orientated venues in the Cathedral Quarter especially, mostly directed towards, young, single gay men.

## Gay bars and clubs

**Custom House**, at The Crow's Nest, 22-8 Skipper St, **T** 9024 5558. *1100-2300 daily. Map 2, E9, p249* One of the longest-standing gay bars in Belfast, on the fringes of the Cathedral Quarter, the Crow's Nest is ideal for daytime city centre drinking. By night it's very crowded but is ideally situated for starting off the evening before moving on to the nearby clubs. Karaoke and Quiz nights.

**Kremlin**, 96 Donegall St, **T** 9080 9700, www.kremlin-belfast.com. *Map 2, C8, p249* A vastly extravagant club with a huge statue of Lenin outside. It is the largest gay venue in Ireland and attracts people from all over the island. It opened its doors to the gay and lesbian citizens of Belfast in March 1999 and since then has firmly established itself. Decor reflects Cold War Russia. Saturday sees *Revolution* with DJs including Stevey Walker and Regal MC Robert May. Atmosphere from camp disco-pop in the club bar, to the latest house, commercial and garage in the club room. Pop videos in Tsar Lounge, a more relaxed alternative to the bar and club. Women are equally welcome here.

**The Kube** 2-16 Dunbar St, **T** 9023 4520, www.kubeonline.com. *Mon-Thu 1130-0100, Fri 1130-0200, Sat 1130-0300, Sun 1900-midnight. Lunch till 1500 most days. Club entrance £5-7. Map 2, D9, p249* The Kube, formerly the Parliament, has a cosy feel to the bar downstairs and a nightclub, *Club Heat*, upstairs. Lunch menu ranges from soup and sandwiches to steak, fish and curry dishes – typical pub grub. DJs and various club nights most nights of the week keep the Kube busy into the early hours. Karaoke is also a perennial favourite. Thu night in the bar is a drag cabaret. Free entry.

**Union St Bar**, Union St, T9031 6060, www.unionstreetpub.com. Restaurant Mon-Wed, Thu 1230-1500, 1700-2000, Fri 1200-2000, Sat 1300-1600. Bar daily 1100-0100. *Map 2, C8, p249* The Union Street Pub and Restaurant is in a converted 19th century shoe factory laid out over three floors. The downstairs area is a busy bar serving food during the day, with open fires and better than the regular pub food. Saturday sees an all night long club night called *Event Horizon*.

## Gay nights in Belfast bars

Some pubs and clubs have dedicated gay nights. Check out www.gaybelfast.net.

**Milk**, (see p161). Monday is Forbidden Fruit with Titti Von Tramp. Admission £5 All drinks £1.50.

**Mono Café bar**, 100 Ann St. *Map 2, E10, p249* Dedicates its Thu nights to a gay evening called *Attitude*.

**The Pavilion**, 296 Ormeau Rd, **T** 9064 0914. *Map 1, G5, p246* Has a gay night on the first Fri of each month called Howl.

Other gay-friendly bars are: **Queen's Bar**, 4 Queen's Arcade; **Apartment** (see p157); **Opium** , Skipper St; and the **John Hewitt** (see p160).

## Organizations and helplines

**Belfast Lesbian Helpline**, **T** 9023 8668. *Thu 0730-2200.*

**Cara-friend** has a gay helpline, **T** 9032 2023. *Mon-Wed 0730-2200.*

**Gay Lesbian Youth Northern Ireland (GLYNI)**, *Cara-friend*, Cathedral Buildings, 64 Donegall St, admin@glyni.org.uk. *Map 4, B3, p252* Meets every Mon.

**Northern Ireland Gay Rights Association**, PO Box 44, Belfast BT1 1SH, **T** 9066 4111. Meets on the first Thu of each month. The social group for lesbian and bisexual women meets at Cara-friend on the third Sun of each month.

**QueerSpace**, Cara-Friend Rooms, Cathedral Buildings, 64 Donegall St, www.queerspace.org.uk. *Map 4, B3, p252* A a volunteer-led organization which serves the lesbian, gay, bisexual and transgendered community of Belfast and Northern Ireland by raising its visibility, supporting its activities, providing resources and facilitating communication, while adhering to the principles of community orientation, freedom of identity, ethical funding and accessibility.

**The Rainbow Project**, manager@rainbow-project.org. Belfast: 2-6 Union St, BT1 2JF, **T** 9031 9030. *Mon-Thu, 1400-1700. Derry: 37 Clarendon St, BT48 7ER,* **T** *7128 3030. Mon, Tue 1000-1400, Wed- Fri 1000-1700.* Promotes sexual health among gay men and has drop in centres in Belfast and Derry.

## Saunas

**The Garage**, 2-6 Union St, info@garage-belfast.com. *Mon 1200-1700, Tue, Wed 1200-0300, Thu 1200- 0400, Fri-Mon 24 hours. £12. Map 2, C8, p249* Steam Room, jacuzzi, video lounge, rest rooms, tea and coffee bar. Grab a drink and mingle with other clients.

## Websites

**www.belfastpride.com**, is the website of the Gay Pride Week which takes place in early August. Events include a parade, river boat trips, disco evenings and quizzes at the various gay centric venues in town (see p180).

**www.foylefriend.org**. A website under construction serving the gay community in Derry.

**www.gaybelfast.net**. A website which covers Belfast events and sights for gay visitors.

**www.menofthenorth.com**. An alternative Belfast venue for gay men over 25 (singles and couples) who want to meet in a relaxed atmosphere. They meet regularly at the Crow's Nest (see Clubs above).

**www.outnabout-ni.org.uk**. The website of a gay and lesbian walking group which holds regular walks around the north.

**www.pinkpages.org**. Website covering gay and lesbian related sites and events. A little out of date for Belfast.

Young visitors to Belfast can have a good time in the city. It is safer and more child-orientated in recent years with sights such as W5, the zoo and the Ulster Museum catering particularly for children. Just outside the city is the amazing Ulster Folk and Transport Museum which will keep tiny minds happy for hours. The city has lots of green spaces for walks and other fair weather activities, an increasing number of leisure centres, and lots of spectator sports to occupy them. Belfast is also close to the seaside and countryside which offers offering amusement arcades, beaches, boat and train rides, a scary rope bridge, old castles to explore, an aquarium, an open working farm and more. The Belfast City Bus Tour (p24) will take the strain out of seeing the city's major sights or you could take a river trip with the Lagan Boat Company (p26) to see where the Titanic was built. Halloween especially is good fun in Northern Ireland where there is a long tradition of celebrating with ghost stories, parties and dressing up. The summer is filled with one event or another and the Belfast Festival caters to local children and visitors alike.

# Activities

**Belfast**

**Dundonald International Ice Bowl**, 111 Old Dundonald Rd, Belfast, **T** 9080 9100, www.theicebowl.com. *Ice rink: Mon-Thu 1100-1700, 1930-2200, Fri 1100-1700, 1730-2200, Sat, Sun 1000-1200, 1300-1700,1730-2200. Ulsterbus 511 from Laganside Bus Centre. Adult £4, children £3, skate hire £1.* Olympic sized ice rink, bowling alley and indoor adventure playground.

**Odyssey Bowl**, Odyssey Pavilion, **T** 9046 7030, www.odyssey bowl.com. *Map 2, C12, p249* 20 lane bowling alley, video games.

**Pickie Family Fun Park**, The Promenade, Bangor, County Down, **T** 9185 7030. *Oct-Easter Daily 1000-sunset, Easter-Oct 1000-2200. Half hourly train from Belfast Central, 30 mins. Swans £2.50, tram £1.25, go-kart £1.25. Map 6, F8, p254* Swan pedal boats, paddling pool, mini-railway, playground, go-carts. Boat trips around the bay.

**Sheridan Imax Cinema**, The Odyssey Pavilion, **T** 90467014, www.belfastimax.com. *Closed Wed. Various show times. Adult £5, child £4. Citybus 600 from Donegall Sq East. Map 2, C12, p249* Giant 6 storey 3D screen, surround sound movies.

# Festivals

**Belfast**

**Young at Art** is a week long child orientated festival held in late October to accompany the Belfast Festival (see p182), featuring

Kids

theatre, art courses, circus, puppetry, storytelling and much more. Bookings in person from festival House, 25 College Gardens, **T** 9097 2626, www.belfastfestival.com.

# Sights

**Belfast**

**Aunt Sandra's Candy Factory**  60 Castlereagh Rd, **T** 9073 2868, www.irishcandyfactory.com. *Mon-Fri 0930-1630, Sat 0930-1700. Closed Sun. Free. Citybus 32. (See p54)  Map 1, F7, p247*  Watch the candy rolled out and squidged into shape and then buy your own - severed fingers and eyeballs at Halloween, giant blue feet all year round, chocolates to take back to grandma, honeycomb, lollies.

**Belfast Zoo**   *Open Apr-Sep, 1000-1800 daily; Oct-Mar 1000-1530. Summer £6.70, winter £5.70. (See p64)  Map 6, F7, p254*  Set in the hills north of the city the zoo offers views back to the city, a cute train to take you to the top, an adventure playground, feeding times and the zoo farm. Add on the monkeys and the baby animals and this makes for a great kid oriented day out.

**Ulster Folk and Transport Museum**, Cultra, **T** 9042 8428, www.magni.org.uk. *Jul and Aug, Mon-Sat, 1000-1800, Sun, 1100-1800; Apr-Jun , Mon-Fri, 1000-1700, Sat, 1000-1800, Sun, 1100-1800; Oct-Mar, Mon-Fri, 1000-1600, Sat 100-1700, Sun, 1100-1700. Last admission 1 hr before closing time. £5, combined ticket to Folk Museum and Transport Museum £6.50. Tea room. Trains and buses to Bangor stop at Cultra, 7 miles (11 km) east of Belfast. (See p66)  Map 6, F7, p254*  One of the best days out in the north regardless of your age, this place has old fashioned schoolrooms, sweetshops, farms, exhibitions of cooking, lace making, spinning and weaving, printing and lots more. A miniature railway adds to the fun.

Kids

## W5
*Hours of constructive things to do...*

**Ulster Museum** *Open Mon-Fri, 1000-1700, Sat 1300-1700, Sun, 1400-1700. Free. Exhibitions change regularly. (See p50)* Map 3, E7, p251 Dinosaurs, mummies, native Americans, sunken galleons, computers, knobs to press, activity packs and more.

**W5**, Odyssey, 2 Queen's Quay, BT39QQ, **T** 90467700, www.w5online.co.uk. *Open daily Mon-Fri 1000-1800, Sat and Sun 1200-1800. Last admission 1700. £5.50. (See p46)* Map 2, C12, p249 W5 has hours of constructive things to do: building model racing cars, discovering gravity, watching a volcano erupt, making cloud rings, playing with computers, cheating a lie detector, checking how healthy, clever, musical or dextrous you are. And the kids can enjoy it too!

**Kids**

## Around the north of Ireland

**Bundoran**. 22 km south of Donegal town Bundoran is a little gem of a seaside town dedicated to family fun. Worth staying for a day or two if you have children Bundoran has lots of accommodation, two beautiful beaches, an outdoor centre, amusement arcades, a fun fair and **Waterworld** (**T** 0724 1172, *Easter-Sep*) an aqua-playground for children with wave pool, slide pool and rapids as well as **Bundoran Glowbowl** (**T** 0719842111) a 10-pin bowling centre with 8 lanes.

**Carrick-a-rede rope bridge**, **T** 2073 1159, 2073 1582. *Open (weather permitting) mid-Mar to Jun and Sep, daily 1000-1800; Jul-Aug, daily 1000-1900. £2. Centre and tea-room: Jun-Aug and weekends in May, daily 1200-1800. (See p88) Map 6, B5, p254* A very quick stop in a day's visit to the north Antrim coast this is well worth seeking out for the thrill of seeing your kids suspended 80ft above the swirling water. Nice views from the bridge if you dare to look.

**Causeway School Museum**, Giant's Causeway Centre, **T** 2073 177. *Daily Jul, Aug 1100-1700. £0.75, child £0.50. (See p85) Map 6, B5, p254* Set in an old national school this offers the experience of schooling in the olden days with funny joined up desks and chairs inkwells, yo-yos, marbles and skipping ropes.

**Downpatrick Steam Railway**, Market St, **T** 44615779, www.downpatricksteamrailway.co.uk. *Trains run from Jul-mid-Sep, 1400-1700, Sat and Sun, only. Also St Patrick's Day, Easter Sun and Mon, Hallowe'en weekend, Dec weekends, 1400-1700. Workshop and Station House: Jun-Sep, Mon-Sat, 1100-1400. (See p72.) Map 6, H8, p255*

**Dunluce Centre**, Sandhill Dr, Portrush, **T** 7082 4444. *Weekends only in Sep-May, daily in Jun Jul and Aug. (See p84) Map 6, B4,* *p254* A themed and zoned interactive games environment with a computerized treasure hunt, and an SFX turbo ride.

**Exploris Aquarium**, The Ropewalk, Castle St, Portaferry, Co Down, **T** 4272 8062, www.exploris.org.uk. *Mon-Fri 1000-1800, Sat 1100-1800, Sun 1300-1800. Closes one hour earlier Sep-Easter. Adult £6.50, child £3.75, family £17.50. Ulsterbus 9A, 10. 1hr 15 mins. Map 6, H8, p255* Aquarium and seal sanctuary with displays of marine life from Strangford Lough. Shallow tanks allow visitors to touch many of the exhibits.

**Giant's Causeway**, Giant's Causeway Centre, **T** 2073 1582. *Open Jul-Aug, daily 1000-1900. Shorter hours rest of the year. Audio-visual show £1. Car-park £5. Tea-room open mid-Mar to Nov. There is no charge to visit the Giant's Causeway unless arriving by car or wishing to hop in the minibus, £.20 return, from the Causeway Centre to the shore. (See p85) Map 6, B5, p254* Ignore the visitor centre and the car park and just take the children out on to the rocks and let them explore the strange formations. Watersports in Portrush.

**Streamvale Open Farm**, 38 Ballyhanwood Rd, Dundonald, to the east of Belfast, **T** 9048 3244, www.streamvale.com. *Daily Easter-end August, Adult £4.20, child £3.75. Citybus 21. Map 6, F8, p254* Working dairy farm with chickens and sheep to feed, milking to watch, pony rides, tractors, strawberries to pick and a marked wildlife walk.

**Waterworld**, Harbour, Portrush, **T** 7082 2001. *£4.50 but family tickets also available; open daily. Map 6, B4, p254* A water playground with all the works as well as a bowling alley and sauna.

**Kids**

# Sleeping and eating

## Belfast

Northern Ireland still allows smoking in public places although many restaurants at least have non-smoking areas. Good child-friendly restaurants include **Soda Joe's**, **T** 9045 8555, **Hard Rock Café**, **T** 9076 6990, **Indian Ocean** (p134) and the **Titanic Grill** (p136), all at the Odyssey Pavilion. **Morelli's Ice Cream Shop**, 329 Ormeau Rd, **T** 9064 3233, sells a vast range of home made ice cream while the **Revelations Internet Café** (p143) has games and is kid friendly. **Day's Hotel** (p110) and the **Travelodge** (p110) both make good financial sense when travelling with children.

Directory

## Banks

**Bank of Ireland**, 54 Donegall Pl, **T** 9023 4334. Linked with Barclays. **Northern Bank**, Donegall Sq West, **T** 9024 5277. **Ulster Bank**, 47 Donegall Pl, **T** 9024 4112. Linked with Natwest. Banking hours are Mon-Fri, 0930-1630, Sat (some banks) 0930-1230.

## Bicycle hire

**McConvey Cycles**, 467 Ormeau Rd, **T** 9033 0322. Bikes for £10 per day, £40 per week, with a deposit of £30. **Life Cycles**, 36-7 Smithfield Market, **T** 9043 9959, www.lifecycles.co.uk. Hires for £9 per day, £40 per week and also does repairs. The tourist office has details of some possible cycle tours of the region.

## Car hire

**Avis**, 69 Great Victoria St, **T** 9024 0404; Belfast International Airport **T** 9442 2333; City Airport, **T** 9045 2017, www.avis.co.uk. **Budget**, 96-102 Gt Victoria St, **T** 9023 0700; Belfast International Airport **T** 9442 3332; City Airport **T** 9045 1111, www.budget-Ireland.co.uk. **Dan Dooley**, 175 Airport Rd, Crumlin, Co Antrim, **T** 9445 2522, 0800-282189, www.dandooley.com. **Europcar**, Belfast International Airport **T** 9442 3444; City Airport **T** 9045 0904, www.europcar.com. **Hertz**, Belfast International Airport, **T** 9442 2533, www.hertz.co.uk.

## Dentists

For emergency treatment seek advice at your accommodation or try the Yellow Pages. National health treatment is available at some dentists but in an emergency you are more likely to find private dentists available.

## Disabled travellers

Websites for disabled visitors: **www.sharevillage.org**, a holiday village for disabled visitors, friends and family; **www.idgss.co.uk/dsni**, a website covering activities in Northern

Ireland for the disabled; **www.disabilityaction.org**, the
Disability Action website; **www.adf.com**, arts and disability
forum. **Ulsterbus** are in the process of introducing low floor
access buses to the city fleet and most of the buses which link bus
and train stations with the main shopping centres have these
buses. A guide to accessible transport in northern Ireland is
available from the **Transport Advisory Committee**, Portside
Business Park, 189 Airport Rd West, **T** 9029 7882,
www.nitran.org.uk.

## Doctors

Citizens of the EU, Iceland, Norway and Liechtenstein are entitled to
free medical treatment in Northern Ireland, although they will have
to pay a prescription charge of £6.40 per item. The availability of free
medical assistance to other nationals varies according to each
country's reciprocal agreements with the UK. All Accident and
Emergency treatment is free to all. **Contacters**, 16 Wellington Park,
BT96JD, **T** 9066 8246, offers an emergency 24 hour service and will
put callers in touch with the nearest available doctor at any time.
You could also ask at your accommodation for a recommendation.
Other surgeries to try for an appointment are: **Drs Hamilton and
Boyd**, 436 Lisburn Rd, BT9 6GR, **T** 9066 7595; or **Dr J M Fitch**, 2
Lower Cres, BT7, **T** 9032 0919.

## Embassies and consulates

**Canada**, 378 Stranmillis Rd, BT9 5ED, **T** 9066 0212. **Denmark**, 1
Corry Pl, Belfast Harbour Estate, BT3 9AH, **T** 9035 0000. **Finland**,
25 Cherryhill, Rostrevor, Co Down, BT34 3B2, **T** 4173 8493. **Greece**,
**Norway**, **Portugal**, at M F Ewings, (Shipping) Ltd, Hurst House,
15-19 Corporation Sq, BT1 3AJ, **T** 9024 2242. **Italy**, 7 Richmond
Park, BT9 5EP, **T** 9066 8854. **Netherlands**, 14-16 West Bank Rd,
BT3 9JL, **T** 9037 0223. **New Zealand**, The Balance House, 118A
Lisburn Rd, BT29 4 NY, **T** 92648098. **Sweden**, G Heyn & Sons Ltd,
Head Line Buildings, 10 Victoria St, BT1 3GP, **T** 9023 0581.

**Switzerland**, 8 The Horse Port, Boneybefore, Carrickfergus, BT38 7EP, **T** 90321626. **USA**, Consulate General, Danesfort House, 223 Stranmillis Rd, BT9 5GR, **T** 90386100.

## Emergency numbers
For **police**, **fire**, **ambulance** dial 999. **Rape Crisis Centre** **T** 9024 9696. **Samaritans**, **T** 0845-7909090. **Victim support**, **T** 9024 4039

## Genealogical research
The **Belfast General Register Office**, Oxford House, 49 Chichester St, Belfast, BT1 4HL, **T** 9025 2000, will arrange for searches to be made of births, marriages or deaths in Northern Ireland before 1922. **The Public Record Office of Northern Ireland**, 66 Balmoral Av, Belfast BT9 6NY, **T** 9025 1318, www.proni.nics.gov.uk, does not conduct research but visitors can make their own searches there.

## Hospitals
Accident and Emergency services are at: **Belfast City Hospital**, Lisburn Rd, **T** 9032 9241; **Mater Hospital**, Crumlin Rd, **T** 9074 1211; **Royal Victoria Hospital**, Grosvenor Rd, **T** 9024 0503; and **Ulster Hospital**, Dundonald, **T** 9048 4511.

## Internet/email
**Revelations Café**, Bradbury Pl, **T** 9032 0337, info@revelations.co.uk. **Belfast Welcome Centre**, 47 Donegall Pl. Mon-Sat 0730-1000. **Linen Hall Library**, Donegall Sq. Mon-Fri 0930-1730 (2030 Thu), Sat 0930-1600. Several hostels have internet access for their guests. British Telecom booths are placed around Donegall Sq and in W5 in the Odyssey Complex. 10p per minute (50p minimum charge).

## Laundry
**Globe Drycleaning and Launderette**, 37 Botanic Av.

## Left luggage
There are no left luggage facilities as yet at the airports or at any of the bus and train stations. There are daytime only left luggage facilities at the **Belfast Welcome Centre**, 47 Donegall Pl, **T** 9024 6609, www.gotobelfast.com.

## Libraries
**Belfast Central Library**, Royal Av, **T** 9050 9150. Mon and Thu 0930-2000, Tue, Wed, Fri 0930-1730, Sat 0930-1300. **Linen Hall Library**, Donegall Sq, **T** 9032 1707. Mon-Fri 0930-1730 (2030 Thu), Sat 0930-1600.

## Lost property
**T** 9065 0222, the police exchange number in Belfast. They will give instructions on how to proceed.

## Media
**Newspapers**  In addition to the British and Irish newspapers which are readily available in newsagents, look out for the Protestant/Unionist tabloid *News Letter* and the pro-nationalist *Irish News*. The *Belfast Telegraph* is a good daily with a liberal/soft unionist bias. Also available is the daily *The Scotsman*. There is also the free monthly *Big List*, available from cafés, bus stations, the Welcome Centre.

**Magazines**  Besides all the usual stuff that is available in Britain, look out for the free monthly *Fate* available at the airports and cafés etc. Chiefly an entertainment guide it has some interesting articles on local enterprise/ music etc.

**Radio**  *BBC Radio Ulster* broadcasts on FM92.4-95.4 and will give you a good insight to the politics of the north. *BBC Radio Foyle* FM931 is also worth listening to in Derry. *RTE Radio 1* broadcasts on FM88.2-90, 95.2 and focuses on news and high-brow entertainment. Can be a great laugh when the latest political scandal in Dublin breaks out.

### Pharmacies

**Boots the Chemist**, 35-47 Donegall Pl, BT1 1DD, **T** 9024 2332. Mon-Wed 0900-1800, Thu 0900-2000, Fri 0900-1800, Sat 0900-1800, Sun 1300-1800. **McBrierly & Sorley**, 27 Ferryquay St, Derry, BT48 6JS, **T** 71263334, Mon-Wed 0900-1800, Thu 0900-2100, Fri 0900-2100, Sat 0900-1800, Sun 1300-1800.

### Police

In an emergency dial 999. Tourist problems should be taken to the Musgrave Police Station in Ann St.

### Public holidays

New Year's Day, January 1. St Patrick's Day, March 17. Good Friday, Friday before Easter Sunday. Easter Monday, Monday following Easter Sunday. May Holidays, first and last Mondays in May. July Holiday, July 12. August Holiday, last Monday in August. Christmas Day, December 25. St Stephen's Day, December 26.

### Taxi companies

**Able Taxis T** 90241999. **City Cabs T** 9024 2000. **Fon a cab T** 9023 3333. Black taxis take several passengers at a time and their prices compare well with the buses. See also Taxi tours p24.

### Telephone

When dialling Northern Ireland from the Republic, the code is 048 followed by an 8 digit number. **Directory Enquiries**, **T** 118500. **International Directory Enquiries T** 153. **Operator Assistance T** 100. **International operator assistance T** 155.

### Transport enquiries

**Translink**, **T** 9066 6630, www.translink.co.uk. Information on Ulsterbus services in the north, train services in the north and Citybus services in Belfast.

# A sprint through history

| | |
|---|---|
| **1177** | Gaelic chieftains the O'Neils build a castle on the banks of the River Farsett. |
| **1566** | An English garrison is established in the settlement of Derry, a small town which has existed since medieval times. |
| **1608** | The English are driven out of Derry. |
| **1613** | Belfast, now the size of a small town, is granted a royal charter under the rule of Baron Arthur Chichester. Scottish and English settlers are encouraged to come to Ulster. |
| **1641** | The local population of Belfast rebels against the Scottish and English settlers. |
| **1682** | The Long Bridge is built over the River Lagan bringing more trade to Belfast. |
| **Late 1600s** | Protestant Huguenots fleeing persecution in France bring their traditional industry of linen-making to Belfast. |
| **1688** | The siege of Derry, where Catholic troops loyal to James II try to enter the city and are locked out by the city's apprentice boys. |
| **1690** | William of Orange arrives in the city on his way to the Battle of the Boyne. |
| **1700** | Belfast is the fourth largest town in Ireland. |
| **1791** | The United Irishmen, a cross-denominational nationalist organization, is formed in Belfast. |
| **1795** | The Orange Order is founded. |

| 1798 | Insurgencies by United Irishmen in Ulster are put down and its leaders flee or are executed. |
|------|---|
| 1820s | Protestant clubs form in Belfast and begin a tradition of parades. Members bear arms and sing anti-Catholic songs. |
| 1829 | Catholic emancipation in Ireland. Riots across the city as Orange parades are banned. |
| 1842 | The first elected town council meets in Belfast. The population reaches 70,000. |
| 1849 | The island-wide potato famine brings hundreds of starving peasants of both religions into Belfast and Derry in search of food and work. |
| 1857 | Riots in the streets of Belfast as Protestant and Catholic mobs fight one another. |
| 1864 | More riots close factories in Belfast. |
| 1867 | Extension of the franchise gives more of the Catholic poor the right to vote. |
| 1886 | The Home Rule being discussed in the British parliament causes more riots in Belfast during which 30-50 people die. |
| 1891 | Population reaches 350,000, larger than Dublin. |
| 1911 | Home Rule for Ireland again comes under discussion in Britain. The Ulster Volunteer Force is formed, its aim to fight for independence for Northern Ireland rather than be part of an independent Irish republic. |
| 1914 | The outbreak of the First World War brings prosperity to Belfast as demand for home grown food, linen for uniforms and warships grows. 1000 Ulster men die in the Battle of the Somme. |

| 1918 | First World War ends and thousands of men return to unemployment. |
|---|---|
| 1920 | Catholics are driven out of all work in the shipbuilding industry. The B Specials are formed, a part-time armed police force made up entirely of Protestants. |
| 1921 | The island of Ireland is divided into the 6 counties of Northern Ireland which are given Home Rule and the 26 counties of Southern Ireland are given dominion status. |
| 1922 | More riots as IRA (see p236) forces attack Protestant homes and factories around Ulster. |
| 1937 | The new constitution of the Republic of Ireland claims sovereignty over Northern Ireland. |
| 1939 | The Republic of Ireland remains neutral during Second World War while the north, and in particular Derry and Belfast, become a vital part of the Allied operations. |
| 1941 | Belfast becomes a target for the German Luftwaffe. |
| 1942 | American troops are stationed in Belfast which increases IRA attacks within the province. |
| 1945 | Suppression of paramilitary activity brings all IRA activity to an end in both the north and the south. The end of the Second World War brings depression back to Northern Ireland and the city of Derry has an unemployment rate 10 times higher than the rest of the United Kingdom. |
| 1956 | The IRA re-emerges and begins a border campaign. In retaliation both British and Irish governments introduce imprisonment without trial. |

| 1968 | The civil rights movement begins first in Derry and then throughout the province. |
|---|---|
| 1969 | British troops are sent into Northern Ireland. The Provisional IRA secedes from the official IRA. |
| 1970 | The SDLP (Social Democrat and Labour Party) is formed to fight for Catholic civil rights. |
| 1971 | The first British soldier dies in Northern Ireland. Internment without trial is reintroduced and hundreds of suspected IRA supporters including Gerry Adams are imprisoned indefinitely. |
| 1972 | 'Bloody Sunday': 13 unarmed civil rights demonstrators are shot dead by the British army. Direct Rule is imposed on Northern Ireland. |
| 1974 | The British government establishes a power-sharing executive body of Northern Ireland with both Protestant and Catholic members. Protestant groups go on strike. The executive is dissolved. IRA attacks kill people on the British mainland. |
| 1981 | Ten IRA prisoners die on hunger strike demanding the right to be considered political prisoners. |
| 1985 | The Anglo-Irish Agreement brings a degree of power-sharing to Northern Ireland but Protestant organizations make the city unworkable and the Agreement is abandoned. |
| 1988 | A lone gunman attacks and kills mourners at an IRA funeral in the Milltown cemetery. |
| 1993 | Secret talks begin between John Hume and Gerry Adams aimed at finding terms for a peace process. Representatives of the British government also take part in secret talks. |

| 1994 | The IRA declares a ceasefire. It lasts for 18 months. |
|------|------|
| 1995 | Several very contentious Orange Order marches are banned throughout Ulster. |
| 1997 | A new government in Britain. The IRA declares a ceasefire again. The possibility of peace talks is again in the air. Both major unionist parties oppose any kind of peace negotiations. Around the province the Parades Commission acts to reroute or ban Orange marches. |
| 1998 | The Good Friday Agreement is drawn up. In referendums both the populations of the north and south approve the agreement. |
| 1999 | A power sharing assembly meets for the first time at Stormont. |
| 2000 | The Assembly is suspended following the failure of agreement over arms decommissioning. |
| 2002 | After a brief reinstatement the assembly is again suspended. |
| 2004 | Agreement fails at the last moment in the latest effort to restore a power sharing Assembly. |
| 2005 | The latest round of negotiations fail over the DUP's demand for photographic evidence of arms decommissioning. The Northern Ireland police authority declares the IRA responsible for the robbery of the Northern Bank in Belfast in December 2004. Following allegations of IRA members' involvement in the stabbing and beating to death of Robert McCartney, Sinn Féin finds itself under greater political pressure than ever. All hope of a settlement seems lost. |

# Art and architecture

| | |
|---|---|
| **6800-6600 BC** | Mount Sandel Co Derry. A community of middle stone age people build a series of round huts measuring 6 m (20 ft) in diameter. The earliest known traces of human building activity in Ireland. |
| **3200 BC** | Ballynagilly, Co Tyrone. Neolithic community builds a rectangular house, its walls made of split planks. |
| **2500 BC** | Newgrange passage tomb is built in County Meath, the first known building in Ireland to be decorated with art. |
| **2000 BC** | In Beaghmore Co Tyrone, several stone circles are erected, probably with the purpose of observing the stars. |
| **3rd century BC** | Goldsmiths are producing La Tène style decorations on gold jewellery such as the gold torque discovered in Broighter, Co Derry, decorated in relief patterns of flowers with a complex clasp. |
| **500-900 AD** | Christian monasteries around Ireland begin producing illuminated manuscripts, such as the Book of Kells. Lay craftsmen produce a multitude of decorated metal, glass and clay objects. |
| **7th-9th centuries** | Series of pillar stones inscribed with crosses and some animal figures erected on the Inishowen Peninsula in Co Donegal. |
| **c700** | A pillarstone is erected in Kilnasaggart, Co Armagh, inscribed in Ogham script, and decorated with images of the cross. |
| **8th century** | Wooden church buildings in place like Armagh are gradually replaced by simple stone buildings. |

| c 9th century | As in the rest of Ireland sandstone high crosses carved with scenes from the Bible and inscriptions requesting prayers for the men who built them are erected at Donaghmore and Arboe in Co Tyrone. |
| --- | --- |
| 10th-12th centuries | A series of round towers are built beside many stone churches across the island. |
| 1140 | A complex basilica-style church is built by St Malachy at Bangor, Co Down, the first of its kind in Ireland. |
| 12-13th centuries | The Norman invasion of Ireland brought the Gothic style of architecture to Irish churches. |
| 1616 | Donegal Castle, a fortified house, is built featuring highly ornate carved chimneypieces. |
| 1618 | Monea Castle, a fortified house, in Co Fermanagh is typical of the domestic architecture of the ruling classes. Its style Scottish in keeping with the ideas of the Scots settlers who constructed it. |
| 1633 | Derry cathedral is constructed in the Gothic style. |
| 1668 | A barn-style church, more typical of ordinary church building, is consecrated at Ballinderry, Co Antrim. |
| 1670 | Richhill House in Co Armagh, an unfortified purely domestic building, is typical of the relative peace of the times. It has European influences and approaches a Classical style, more common in the next century. |
| 1737 | The parish church of Newtownbreda in Co Down is designed by Richard Castle, the architect of many of Dublin's grand buildings. |
| 1793 | Castlecoole House in Co Fermanagh is completed, designed by James Wyatt. Palladian in style, as |

many of the grand houses of the 18th century in Ireland were, and built in Portland stone.

**Late 18th century**
Development of Belfast into a city begins under the control of the fifth earl of Donegall. Donegall Place and Donegall Street are built as part of a grid pattern. Many buildings designed by the local architect Roger Mulholland. Towns such as Derry, Coleraine and Clones are laid out around a central diamond or square.

The Ulster born artist Robert Hunter is active in Dublin, producing portraits of landed gentry.

**1780s**
A cut glass glass factory is set up in Belfast.

**1817**
Peter Turnerelli (1774-1839), Belfast-born sculptor creates the monument to Father Betagh in Saints Michael and John Church, Arran Quay, Dublin.

**Early 19th century**
Many Ulster churches are built in the neo-classical style eg Portaferry Presbyterian Church consecrated in 1840 and designed by John Millar (1812-76). The entrance to the church has rows of Doric columns, topped by a frieze and pediment.

**1839-40**
The Palm House in Belfast's Botanic gardens is erected preceding Dublin's Glasnevin glasshouses of 1842.

**1846**
Ballywalter Park in Co Down is designed by Sir Charles Lanyon in Italian style.

**1850**
A design school is set up in Belfast.

**1856**
Birth of Sir John Lavery an internationally acclaimed Belfast portrait painter.

**1857**
The Custom House in Belfast is built, designed by Sir Charles Lanyon in the Italian style.

| | |
|---|---|
| **1860s** | The Belleek factory is established in Co Fermanagh making delicate porcelain objects. |
| **1868-70** | Belfast castle is built in a Scottish baronial style. Designed by Sir Charles Lanyon. |
| **1876** | Birth of Paul Henry in Belfast. Later became internationally known for his paintings of the west of Ireland. |
| **1881** | Birth of William Conor in Belfast. Later an official war artist of the First World War. |
| **1887** | Birth of James Dixon on Tory Island, Co Donegal. Later to become one of the island's group of primitive painters. |
| **Late 19th century** | Most of the impressive buildings around Donegall Square are erected, designed by W H Lynne, Young and Mackenzie, Lanyon and Isaac Farrell. |
| **1896** | Construction of St Anne's Cathedral begins, based on designs by Thomas Drew, W H Lynne, and others. |
| **1903** | Birth of Nora McGuinness in Derry. Later illustrator and painter of cubist style still life. |
| **1906** | The Victorian City Hall, designed by Alfred Brumwell Thomas, is opened. |
| **1913** | Birth of William Scott in Enniskillen, Co Fermanagh. Later to become northern Ireland's most significant 20th century painter. |
| **1916** | Birth of Liam McCormick in Derry. He later becomes a groundbreaking architect. |
| **1920s** | Wall murals depicting the Battle of the Boyne and other Protestant icons begin appearing in Derry, |

Belfast and other towns in the north.

| 1927 | Birth of Deborah Brown in Belfast. Later to hold exhibits of her sculpture in Belfast Museum. |
| 1929 | The Belfast Museum and Art Gallery is opened. |
| 1933 | William Conor's painting *Washing Day* captures the atmosphere of working class Belfast. |
| 1939 | Nor McGuinness returns to Ireland from Europe and her work becomes part of the most avant-garde practised in Ireland. |
| 1943 | The Arts Council of Northern Ireland is set up to encourage music and the arts in the province. |
| 1960s | Belfast Museum becomes the Ulster Museum. |
| 1967 | Church of St Aengus, Burt Co Donegal is built in a modern geometric style to a design by Liam McCormick, the Derry-born architect. |
| 1981 | The first Republican wall murals begin to appear in Belfast, Derry and other towns in the north. |
| 1982 | Retrospective of the work of Belfast sculptor Deborah Brown held in the National Museum of Ulster. |
| 1990 | Deborah Brown's sculpture *Sheep on the Road* bought and later displayed at the Waterfront in Belfast. |

# Books

## Fiction

**Deane, Seamus** *Reading in the Dark*. (1997) Vintage. Set in Derry in the 1950s and 60s and reaching into a personal and political heart of darkness.

**MacGill, Patrick** *Children of the Dead End* and *The Rat-Pack*. (2001) New Island Books. Two books, originally published in 1914 and 1915, that tell you more about colonial Ireland than many a history book.

**McLaverty, Michael** *Call My Brother Back*. (1939, 2003) Blackstaff. First published in 1939, this has been acclaimed the best novel out of the north of Ireland.

**Park, David** *Swallowing the Sun*. (2004) Bloomsbury. Gripping contemporary fiction by a Northern Irish writer.

## Non-fiction

**Adams, Gerry** *Falls Memories*. (1993) Brandon. Memories of a working-class community in Belfast by someone who was there.

**Barden, Jonathan** *A History of Ulster*. (2004) Blackstaff. Easily the best history of the northern province, even-handed throughout and in a style that makes it a pleasure to read, and now in a new and updated edition.

**Craig, Patricia** (ed) *The Belfast Anthology*. (1999) Blackstaff. Where else would Gerry Adams, Graham Greene, Philip Larkin and Van Morrison rub shoulders? An anthology of material from the

17th century to the present: memoirs, poetry, fiction, travel writing, history and letters.

**Dillon, Paddy** *The Ulster Way*. (1999) O'Brien Press. The complete Ulster Way written by a noted author of many walking guides.

**Eagleton, Terry** *The Truth About The Irish*. (1999) New Island Books. A laugh a minute, literally, in this alphabet of Irish mores. Worth reading for the entry on B&Bs alone.

**Maguire, WA** *Belfast*. (1993) Ryburn Publishing. A title in a *Town and City Histories* series, charting the rise and long fall of industrial Belfast and social and political developments.

**Mckay, Susan** *Northern Protestant: An Unsettled People*. (2001) Blackstaff. Full of insights into the contradictory nature of the Protestant communities of Northern Ireland; find place in your luggage for this one.

**Sands, Bobby** *Bobby Sands Writings from Prison*. (1998) Mercier. Secretly written and smuggled out from Long Kesh, a painful account of a man's attempt to preserve in prose and poetry his sense of identity.

**Scott, Robert** *Wild Belfast: On Safari in the City*. (2004) Blackstaff. A guide to the wild creatures and plants that inhabit the city.

**Taylor, Peter** *Provos*. (1997) Bloomsbury. An informed journalist writes the best account of how the IRA re-emerged after the events of 1969 and how Sinn Féin rose to power.

**Watson, Philip S** *Companion to the Causeway Coast Way*. (2004) Blackstaff. The Way divided into seven excursions, illustrated in colour, ideal for a day or two away from the metropolis.

## Poetry

**Heaney, Seamus** *North*. (1975) Faber. Heaney's most engaging set of poems as he sets about confronting brute facts regarding colonialism and the social divisions of his country. His mythologizing instinct comes face to face with violence and the poetry reaches new heights.

**Heaney, Seamus** *Opened Ground* (1998) Faber. To date, this is the closest Heaney comes to presenting his *oeuvre*, containing selections from *Wintering Out* (1972), *Stations* and *North* (1975), *Field Work* (1979), *Station Island* (1983), *The Haw Lantern* (1987), *Seeing Things* (1990) and *The Spirit Level* (1996). Enough here to last a lifetime.

**Paulin, Tom** *Selected Poems*. (1993) Faber. Thoughtful, sophisticated but politically engaged poems from a fine Northern Irish writer.

# Glossary

**Alliance Party**  Formed in 1970, a non-sectarian mix of middle-class members of both communities, with seats in the Assembly but none at Westminster

**B Specials**  An auxiliary and highly partisan police force of the Stormont government, abolished in 1971

**Diamond**  town square

**DUP**  The Democratic Unionist Party, led by Ian Paisley, vehemently anti-Republican and until very recently vigorously opposed to the Good Friday Agreement. Now the main non-nationalist party in Northern Ireland

**Éire**  Irish for Ireland

**IRA**  Irish Republican Army. Between 1916 and 1921 the IRA was the army of the Provisional Government fighting the British and relatively dormant until trouble erupted in Northern Ireland at the end of the 1960s. Between 1970 and the still-existing ceasefire called in 1998 the IRA was actively engaged in a guerilla war against the British

**Lough**  a lake

**Loyalists**  people in Northern Ireland, staunch Protestants mostly, who are strongly in favour of remaining part of Britain

**LVF**  Loyalist Volunteer Force. An illegal, loyalist paramilitary group

**Nationalists**  People who wish to see a united Ireland

**North**  shorthand for Northern Ireland

**NITB**  Northern Ireland Tourist Board

**Orange Order**  Protestant society dedicated to preserving the memory of William's victory at the Battle of the Boyne. Founded in 1795 and formerly represented within the Ulster Unionist Party

**Plantation**  term referring to the settlement of the English and Scottish, beginning in the late 16th century in southwest Cork and in the early 17th century in Ulster

**PSNI**  Police Service of Northern Ireland, formerly the Royal Ulster Constabulary, Northern Ireland's armed police force, still predominantly Protestant.

**PUP**  Progressive Unionist Party, the political wing of the UVF, and crucial to the success of the Good Friday Agreement. Led by David Ervine, a moderating force compared to the DUP

**Real IRA**  Formed in 1997 by dissident IRA members who opposed the peace process and the political leadership of Sinn Féin

**Republic**  shorthand for the 26 counties of the Republic of Ireland

**Republicans**  people committed to a united Ireland as a republic; sometimes used interchangeably with the term nationalist

**RUC**  Royal Ulster Constabulary, Northern Ireland's armed police force, predominantly Protestant. Very much a sectarian force until reformed and renamed the Police Service of Northern Ireland (PSNI)

**Sinn Féin**  'Ourselves Alone'. Nationalist organization founded in 1903 and nowadays a political party in Ireland, particularly strong in the North, where it represents the political wing of the IRA. Led by Gerry Adams

**SDLP** Social Democratic and Labour Party, led by John Hume for many years, nationalist but not as republican as Sinn Fein

**Treaty** the Treaty of 1921 that divided Ireland into the Republic and Northern Ireland

**Tricolour** the green, white and orange flag of the Republic of Ireland

**UDA** Ulster Defence Association; Largest Protestant paramilitary organization, formed in 1971

**UDF** Ulster Defence Force, an illegal Protestant paramilitary organization

**UDR** Ulster Defence Regiment, political wing of the LVF

**UFF** Ulster Freedom Fighters; officially non-existant, a Protestant paramilitary force used by the UDA to carry out attacks against republicans

**UUP** The Ulster Unionist Party, led by David Trimble, for years the strongest and most moderate of the unionist parties, currently playing second fiddle to the DUP

**UVF** Ulster Volunteer Force, an illegal Protestant paramilitary force formed in 1966 and supported by several thousand hardliners

**YHANI** Youth Hostel Association of Northern Ireland

# Index

# Credits

### Footprint credits

Editor: Sarah Thorowgood
Map editor: Sarah Sorensen
Picture editor: Kevin Feeney
Publisher: Patrick Dawson
Series created by: Rachel Fielding
In-house cartography: Robert Lunn,
Claire Benison, Kevin Feeney, Angus
Dawson, Esther Monzón, Thom Wickes
Design: Mytton Williams
Maps: Footprint Handbooks Ltd

### Photography credits

Front cover: GoToBelfast.com
Inside: Alamy, GoToBelfast.com (p31
Big Fish, Laganside; p69 Barrel Man,
Laganside), Rory Pearce (p5 detail of
Malmaison), Powerstock, Scenic Ireland
(p1 angel sculpture, Laganside).
Generic images: John Matchett
Back cover: Alamy

### Print

Manufactured in Italy by LegoPrint
Pulp from sustainable forests

### Footprint feedback

Every effort has been made to ensure
that the facts in this pocket guide are
accurate. However, the authors and
publishers cannot accept responsibility
for any loss, injury or inconvenience
sustained by any traveller as a result
of information or advice contained in
this guide. If you want to let us know
about your experiences, go to
www.footprintbooks.com and send
in your comments.

### Publishing information

Footprint Belfast and the north of Ireland
1st edition
Text and maps
© Footprint Handbooks Ltd
April 2005

Maps based upon the Ordnance Survey
Complete Atlas of Ireland, with
permission of the Controller of Her
Majesty's Stationery Office, © Crown
Copyright 2005

ISBN: 1 904777 39 2
CIP DATA: a catalogue record for this
book is available from the British Library

Published by Footprint Handbooks
6 Riverside Court
Lower Bristol Road
Bath, BA2 3DZ, UK
T +44 (0)1225 469141
F +44 (0)1225 469461
discover@footprintbooks.com
www.footprintbooks.com

Distributed in the USA by
Publishers Group West

**Publishing stuff**

# Complete title list

(P) denotes pocket guide

Publishing stuff

## Latin America & Caribbean

Antigua & Leeward
 Islands (P)
Argentina
Barbados (P)
Bolivia
Brazil
Caribbean Islands
Central America & Mexico
Chile
Colombia
Costa Rica
Cuba
Cusco & the Inca Trail
Dominican Republic (P)
Ecuador & Galápagos
Havana (P)
Mexico
Nicaragua
Peru
Rio de Janeiro (P)
South American Handbook
St Lucia (P)
Venezuela

## North America

New York (P)
Vancouver (P)
Western Canada

## Africa

Cape Town (P)
East Africa
Egypt
Libya
Marrakech (P)
Morocco
Namibia
South Africa
Tunisia
Uganda

## Middle East

Dubai (P)
Jordan
Syria & Lebanon

## Australasia

Australia
East Coast Australia
New Zealand
Sydney (P)
West Coast Australia

## Asia

Bali
Bhutan
Cambodia
Goa
Hong Kong (P)
India
Indian Himalaya
Indonesia
Laos
Malaysia
Nepal
Northern Pakistan
Rajasthan
Singapore
South India
Sri Lanka
Sumatra
Thailand
Tibet
Vietnam

## Europe

Andalucía
Barcelona (P)
Berlin (P)
Bilbao (P)
Bologna (P)
Britain
Cardiff (P)
Copenhagen (P)
Croatia
Dublin (P)
Edinburgh (P)
England
Glasgow (P)
Ireland
London (P)
Madrid (P)
Naples (P)
Northern Spain
Paris (P)
Reykjavik (P)
Scotland
Scotland Highlands
 & Islands
Spain
Tallin (P)
Turin (P)
Turkey
Valencia (P)
Verona (P)

## Backpacker

Belize, Guatemala &
 Southern Mexico
Patagonia
Peru, Bolivia & Ecuador

## Lifestyle

Surfing Europe
Surfing Britain

Check out...

# www...

100 travel guides, 100s of destinations, 5 continents
and 1 Footprint...

www.footprintbooks.com

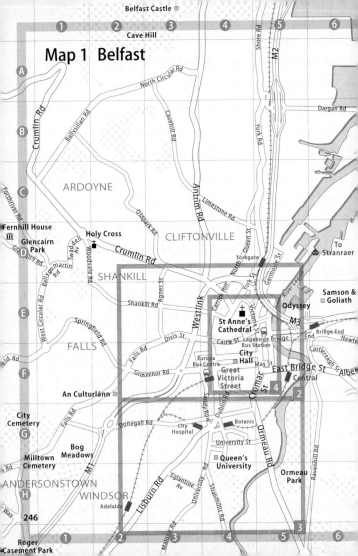

# Map 1  Belfast

Belfast Castle

Cave Hill

North Circular Rd

Crumlin Rd

Ballysillan Rd

Shore Rd

M2

Dargan Rd

Cavehill Rd

ARDOYNE

Antrim Rd

Limestone Rd

CLIFTONVILLE

York Rd

Oldpark Rd

Forthriver Rd

Fernhill House

Glencairn Park

Ballygomartin Rd

Crumlin Rd

Holy Cross

Woodvale Rd

SHANKILL

Agnes St

Westlink

Carrick Hill

North Queen St

Yorkgate

Garmoyle St

River Lagan

To Stranraer

Samson & Goliath

Odyssey

West Circular Rd

Springfield Rd

Shankill Rd

Divis St

St Anne's Cathedral

Victoria St

York St

M3

Bridge End

Castlereagh St

Newte

FALLS

Falls Rd

Falls Rd

Grosvenor Rd

Europa Bus Centre

Great Victoria Street

Castle St

Laganside Bridge
Bus Station

City Hall

May St

Cromac St

East Bridge St

4

Central

2

An Culturlann

Dublin Rd

City Cemetery

Donegall Rd

City Hospital

Botanic

Ormeau Rd

Milltown Cemetery

Bog Meadows

Falls Rd

University St

Queen's University

Ormeau Park

ANDERSONSTOWN

WINDSOR

M1

Lisburn Rd

Adelaide

Eglantine Av

University Rd

Stranmillis Rd

Malone Rd

Ravenhill

Ravenhill Rd

3

246

Roger Casement Park

Way Rd

① ② ③ ④ ⑤ ⑥

Ⓐ Ⓑ Ⓒ Ⓓ Ⓔ Ⓕ Ⓖ Ⓗ

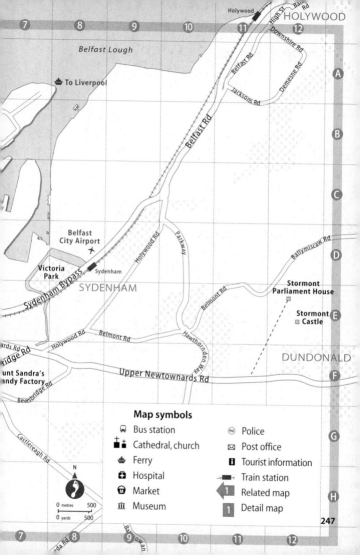

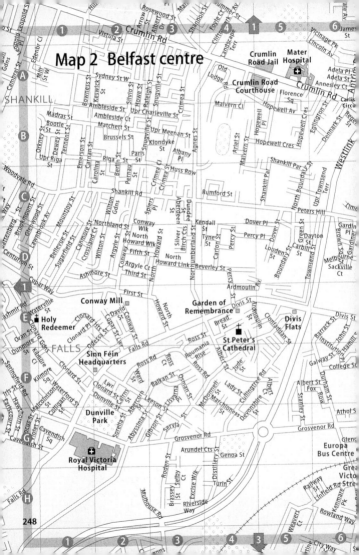

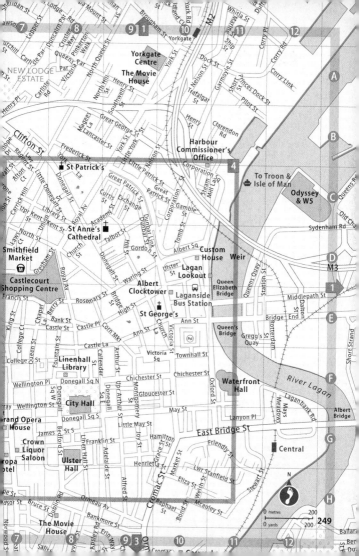

Reldan St
Lodge
Mount St
Brougham St
York St
Midland Cl
York Rd
M2
Whitla St
Dalton
Corry Rd
AWSO St
7
Lepper St
Leon Par. Duncairn St
Crushers Way
Pinkerton Walk
9
1
Yorkgate
10
Ship St
Whitla St
11
Corry Link
12

Churchill Carlisle
New Queen St
Queens Par
Yorkgate Centre
Dock St
Garmoyle St
Princes Dock St
Corry Rd
A

NEW LODGE ESTATE
Victoria Par
North Queen St
North Hill St
Henry St
Little York St
The Movie House
York St
Nelson St
Trafalgar St
Short St
Pilot St
B

Henry Pl
St
Clifton St
Frederick St
Great George's St
York St
Little York
Henry Rd
Clarendon Rd
Corry Link
To Troon & Isle of Man

Library St
Regent St
Donegall St
Lancaster St
Curtis St
Exchange St
Great Patrick St
Dunbar Link
Corporation St
Steam Mill La
Sydenham Rd
Odyssey & W5
Queen's
C

St Patrick's
Donegall St
Academy
Talbot St
Gordo
Albert Sq
Custom House
Weir
Old Cha
M3
D

Carrick Hill
Upr Kent St
Kent St
Royal Av
Church St
Waring St
Ulster St
Lagan Lookout
Queen Elizabeth Bridge
Queen's Quay
Middlepath St
Dalton St
1

Smithfield Market
Gresham St
Royal Av
Donegall St
Bridge St
High St
Albert Clocktower
Laganside Bus Station
Bridge End
E

Castlecourt Shopping Centre
Francis St
Berry St
Rosemary St
St George's
Ann St
Queen's Bridge
Gregg's Quay
Rotterdam
Short Strand

King St
Chapel La
Bank St
Corn Mkt
Victoria St
Ann St
PW
F

College Ct
Castle St
Castle La
Arthur St
Townhall St
River Lagan

Queen St
College Sq
Castle St
Callender St
Chichester St
Oxford St
Waterfront Hall
Laganbank Rd
Albert Bridge

Linenhall Library
Donegall Sq N
Montgomery St
Gloucester St
Mays Meadows
Lanyon Pl
G

Wellington Pl
City Hall
Donegall Sq W
Upr Arthur St
May St
East Bridge St

ray
Wellington St
Donegall Sq S
Little May St
Central

Grand Opera House
James St
Bedford St
Linen Hall St
Hamilton St
Friendly St
Stewart St
H

Crown Liquor Saloon
Franklin St
Adelaide St
Joy St
Market St
N

ropa tel
Ulster Hall
Alfred St
Henrietta St
Eliza St
Welsh St
McAuley St
0 metres 200
0 yards 200
249

pe St
Bruce St
Dublin
The Movie House
Cromac St
Orm
Raphael St
Bond St
Stewart St

Windsor St
7
Norwood
Safir
Apsley St
Erin Way
8
9
3
Orn
10
Cromac
11
12
Ballar

# Map 3  South Belfast

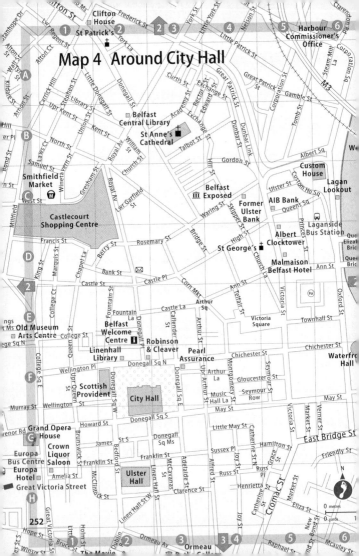

# Map 4  Around City Hall

**A**
- Clifton St
- Lw Regent St
- Hanhope St
- Alton St
- Kildare St
- Arnon St
- Carrick Hill
- Stephen St
- Union St
- Frederick St
- York St
- Little York St
- Nelson St
- York La
- Clifton House
- St Patrick's
- Clarendon Rd

❶ ❷ ❸ ❹ ❺ ❻ Harbour Commissioner's Office
- Corporation Sq
- Steam Mill La
- M3

**B**
- Library St
- Upr Kent St
- North St
- Laws Ct
- Samuel St
- Bomb'd Hill
- Kildare St
- Ler Pl
- Donegall St
- Curtis St
- Academy St
- Exchange St
- Great Patrick St
- Little Patrick St
- Exchange St W
- Rector St
- Edward St
- Corporation St
- Gamble St
- Tomb St
- Belfast Central Library
- St Anne's Cathedral
- Dunbar Link
- Talbot St
- Gordon St
- Hill St
- Skipper St
- Albert Sq
- Custom House
- Lagan Lookout
- We

**C**
- Bomb'd St
- Millfield
- Smithfield Market
- West St
- Wineta St
- Western St
- Church St
- Royal Av
- Gresham St
- Upr Garfield St
- Lwr Garfield St
- Waring St
- Belfast Exposed
- Former Ulster Bank
- AIB Bank
- Ulster St
- Custom Ho Sq
- Queens St
- Prince's St
- Lanaside Bus Station
- Que Eliza Bric
- Que Bric

**D**
- Castlecourt Shopping Centre
- Francis St
- Marquis St
- Chapel La
- Berry St
- Rosemary St
- Bridge St
- High St
- Bank St
- Castle Pl
- Corn Mkt
- St George's
- Albert Clocktower
- Church La
- Malmaison Belfast Hotel
- Ann St
- Victoria St
- Oxford St

**E**
- King St
- College Ct
- Castle St
- Fountain St
- Fountain La
- Castle La
- Arthur St
- Ann St
- Teilfair St
- Arthur Sq
- Victoria Square
- Townhall St
- Pol

**F**
- ngs
- Ms
- Old Museum
- Arts Centre
- College La
- ge Sq N
- College Sq E
- Belfast Welcome Centre
- Robinson & Cleaver
- Linenhall Library
- Donegall Sq N
- Pearl Assurance
- Upr Arthur St
- Arthur La
- Chichester St
- Montgomery St
- Gloucester St
- Seymour St
- Waterfront Hall

**G**
- Grand Opera House
- Wellington Pl
- Upr Queen St
- Scottish Provident
- Murray St
- Wellington St
- City Hall
- Donegall Sq W
- Donegall Sq S
- Howard St
- James St S
- Music Hall La
- Seymour Row
- May St
- Victoria St
- Market St
- Verner St
- East Bridge St

**H**
- Europa Bus Centre
- Europa Hotel
- Great Victoria Street
- Grand Opera House
- Crown Liquor Saloon
- Brunswick St
- Bedford St
- Franklin St
- McClintock St
- Amelia St
- Ulster Hall
- Adelaide St
- McCavanas St
- Clarence St
- Alfred St
- Russ St
- Sussex Pl
- Hamilton St
- Catherine St N
- Joy St
- Grace St
- Russ St
- Henrietta St
- Cromac St
- Eliza St
- New Bond St
- Raphael St
- McAuley St

**252**
- Hope St
- Great Victoria St
- Holm St
- Bruce St
- Dublin Rd
- Ormeau Av
- Ormeau
- Linen Hall St W
- Winsor Rd
- Glengall St

❶ ❷ ❸ ❹ ❺ ❻

0 metres
0 yards

N